ENDORSEMENTS

"Many books, methodologies and/or frameworks are mere shortcuts, loose pieces or hacks of what we want to truly achieve in life. Matt´s methodology takes a different approach and lets you take your own life by the horns and helps you to focus on removing or solving the obstacles and hurdles to find your inner compass and direction, to take your personal and professional life to where you want to go. Matt´s framework changed my life around completely, taking ownership of relationships where initially I had given up and completely gaining the opposite outcome, challenging my own thinking, confronting my life challenges in a constructive manner whilst focusing on a healthy balance of physical and mental wellbeing. It took my life beyond any expectation and made me sit in the driver´s seat to find my own path to life success. For the readers of this book, one cannot obtain the gold without slaying the dragon, the more you can look inward the more you will get out of your own life. This is the beginning of your own personal leadership credo. In the end it all starts and ends with you!"

Pascal Ossevoort:
Head of Digital Sales – Africa SAP

"Jumpstone provides an invaluable service. Matt is down to earth and so easy to talk to, I immediately felt at ease speaking with him about anything and everything regarding my professional development. He was so skilled at focusing on deep underlying issues that were affecting my potential. I have read a lot of self-help books/podcasts etc., and thought I had heard it all, but Matt always surprised me with a new perspective or a new technique to make me see things in a way I hadn't before. I will forever be grateful for this experience as it has truly been life changing. I would recommend this to any colleague/ family/friend who wants to grow professionally and personally."

Lizette Gonzales:
MD Texas Med Clinic

"As part of my leadership development tasks, I had the opportunity to go through a series of individual meetings with Matt. Matt has a fantastic research instinct and fundamental coach knowledge. Matt communicates provocatively but at the same time carefully, gradually plunging into points of special attention and blind zones. In several sessions, Matt was able to identify and focus me on the areas of leadership development that are important and achievable for me, drawing attention not only to the traditional strengths but also to the high potential of converting my weaknesses into auxiliary powers."

Ivan Ryzhkov:
Partner Business Director, EMEA South - SAP

INNER
Compass

INNER Compass

Navigate To Live Your True North

MATT GUIVER

Inner Compass: ***Navigate To Live Your True North***

Jones Media Publishing
10645 N. Tatum Blvd. Ste. 200-166
Phoenix, AZ 85028
www.JonesMediaPublishing.com

Disclaimer:
The author strives to be as accurate and complete as possible in the creation of this book, notwithstanding the fact that he does not warrant or represent at any time that the contents within are accurate due to the rapidly changing nature of the Internet.

While all attempts have been made to verify information provided in this publication, the Publisher assumes no responsibility for errors, omissions, or contrary interpretation of the subject matter herein. Any perceived slights of specific persons, peoples, or organizations are unintentional.

In practical advice books, like anything else in life, there are no guarantees of income made. Readers are cautioned to reply on their own judgment about their individual circumstances to act accordingly. This book is not intended for use as a source of legal, business, accounting or financial advice. All readers are advised to seek services of competent professionals in legal, business, accounting, and finance field.

ISBN: 978-1-948382-38-0 paperback

Printed in the United States of America

DEDICATION

First and foremost, this book is dedicated to my clients for providing the source of inspiration in honing and developing this unique model. This book would not be possible without their openness, trust, and vulnerability in exploring their personal challenges. I am eternally amazed at the clarity and perspective this Pathfinder Model brings, but even more so at the bravery, inspiration, and determination so many of my clients have faced in realizing their dreams.

My wife, Jessica, for providing the love, support, and financial bedrock to allow me to realise my own dream in Jumpstone International.

Nick Malone for being the epitome of a true loyal lifelong friend. His support has been truly legendary during our expeditions of life and adventure. Without his unwavering belief, humour, guidance, and investment in Jumpstone International, I can safely say I would not have made it this far.

I am also eternally grateful for all those I have leaned on; thank you for letting me pick your brains and ask for advice and insight. I have been immensely fortunate to see a lot of the world, meet extraordinary people, and taste adventure in travel, business, and life. And it's these experiences that have enriched my career and provided the valuable perspective that I am able to share with clients today.

Therefore, I dedicate my first book to all those who are trying to find clarity by reaching inside of themselves, exploring their inner calling, and daring to bring their goals and dreams to reality.

ACKNOWLEDGEMENTS

I would like to thank Jeremy Jones at Jones Media Publishing for his patience and guidance in crafting this book. I hit many stumbling blocks and procrastination hurdles along the way and without Jeremy's superb Authority Coach Blueprint program, I would still be staring into the abyss. I would also like to thank the countless suggestions, feedback and insights from all the people I have leaned on in gaining the perspective I needed for my readers.

It is my sincere hope that my first book is worthy of publishing and provides valuable content to aid any individual interested to navigate on a bearing aligned to their true north.

TABLE OF CONTENTS

FOREWORD

There are tons of great pieces of literature and resources out there to help identify one's purpose, better manage oneself, or harness one's goals in life. So much that one can easily get lost. In fact, making sense of one's actions and decisions with a broader rationale is a daunting task that I have personally struggled with for years!

In this insightful and practical read, Matt aims at helping you to live a life aligned with your true north! This is no small task. And, yet, it is surprisingly effective! Importantly, it starts with your context and who you are, a too often overlooked step. It then combines renowned frameworks with practical exercises; in particular, some that smartly tap into your subconscious. Finally, it reconciles both your professional and personal life so that you don't have to constantly choose between the two.

In just a matter of hours, invested over a few weeks, Matt's approach helped me put many pieces together and gain the clarity and confidence needed to lean in and embrace new opportunities.

Arnaud Merlet
CEO, N-SIDE

INTRODUCTION

John Lennon said, "Life happens while you are busy making plans." This is all well and good if your life turns out exciting, adventurous and how you had hoped. *But what if you have that lost and disorientated feeling that things are way off track, and you don't know how to gain your bearings and navigate back onto the right path?* Many of my clients feel exactly this way: lost in the fog of their lives, struggling to know which direction to turn, and just trudging on in hope that things will miraculously turn out better. They often feel trapped by their situations because they don't know if taking the wrong turn will make things even worse, so they reluctantly stay their course knowing things *could* be better, hoping the next corner will bring the path and view they've been searching for.

Now, imagine the *opposite*. You know *exactly* where you are on your life map and can pinpoint your current position in life. You understand the terrain and landscape that you've travelled through, you're happy where you are and admire the view, but you're equally eager to move forward with clarity and direction as you navigate your true path.

Of course, it isn't always easy. For me, there were times when I felt extremely disoriented and totally lost – but it's been a rewarding adventure. Today, after 25 years, I've finally found my true north through a mix of luck and determination, but the key was ultimately clarity. It is my fervent belief that you too can find your true path if you engage with the material found in the chapters of *Inner Compass* and use the Pathfinder Leadership Model to orient your bearing.

This book has been written as a guide to steer you in navigating your true path. There is a lot of truth in Franklin D. Roosevelt's quote, "A **smooth sea never** made a **skilled sailor**," but I'd rather you altogether avoid the turbulent storms that threaten to sink your lifeboat before you find your bearing!

The Inner Compass' internal workings are based on the revolutionary *Pathfinder Model*. It is a unique framework that allows people to orientate themselves and navigate to their aspired position in life. It all came about after Erich (SAP client) asked me to create a model to illustrate how all the dots come together from each of our coaching sessions. Over the course of 3-6 months, Erich had collected so many nuggets, insights, and revelations, he was finding it hard to keep track of them all, unsure of how to place them in context with each other. After several prototypes, the Pathfinder Model came together and today forms the bedrock of Jumpstone International's Leadership Pathfinder Program. The map allows my clients to plot their own unique circumstances; identify where they have clarity and where they need more focus and attention. The model provides a true understanding of the past, a fix on the present, and clues as to the bearing needed for the future. It allows anyone to navigate the path they want to take to realise their aspirations and fulfill their true potential – hence living their true north.

I have created a useful resource page on Jumpstone International's website for any purchaser of the book which profiles the coaching clip videos, models and techniques described throughout the book. Access is password protected for purchasers of the book.

A more detailed close-up of the Leadership Pathfinder Model can be found here:

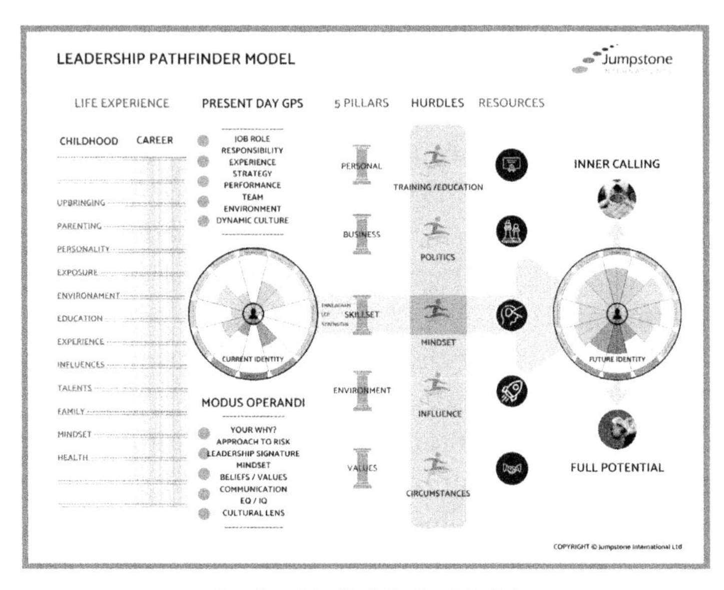

Leadership Pathfinder Model

URL: https://jumpstoneinternational.com/innercompass-resource/

[Website Resource Password: Inner-Compass72!]

The Leadership Pathfinder Model

CONTEXT: The first part illustrates how our context or conditioning through our childhood experience and upbringing shapes how we operate today. It is the root to our modus operandi but essentially it is a mix of nature and nurture combined with our personality and mindset. I take time to listen to my client's 'story' because it gives me context and helps join the dots to whatever is happening in their lives today. Most of us have blind spots or conditioning (much like Pavlov illustrated with his salivating dog experiment) that we have learned through our childhood and beyond. This conditioning can either support or sabotage our endeavours but many of us are often unaware to even be cognisant of it. E3 is a coaching framework I've created to 'Explore your Thinking, Examine your Challenges and Execute on a Plan' which helps you orientate your position and mindset from the outset.

CAREER PATH: The shaded career column illustrates the career path to the present day and attempts to convey the varied nature this can take. Some have had a concise, clear career path within the same company. Others have had a more varied career path, either within the same field or across several industries. There is obviously no right or wrong experience, but it helps to understand the path each individual has taken as it indicates an overall propensity to risk, opportunity, mindset and drive.

PRESENT DAY GPS: The third column represents the present day and how they are currently navigating their life. This top segment represents their current job role and everything it entails. The middle diagram represents the present day snapshot of their wheel of life (a tool that calibrates their position across holistic areas of their life), while the bottom segment represents their interpersonal skills or, as I prefer to call it, 'modus operandi' and how effective they are at leveraging their talents and interpersonal skills to achieve their goals, and realise their aspirations.

5 PILLARS: The five pillars allow an individual to gain true insight into their overarching vision for key areas in their life. I liken it to the Matrix film where Neo steps into the white box. It allows them to imagine their ideal life through constructing their vision around each pillar. My clients are then able to clearly cross-reference back to their current position and compare the reality versus the vision. This allows them to determine what areas they need to focus on and what actions they need to take to make it a reality. I've discovered over many years as an executive coach that far too many people are passive or reactive in steering their lives. They are often reacting to subconscious factors that influence their direction in life, such as family expectations, mindset or career carrots without enough clarity around where and what they are trying to achieve in alignment with their aspirations. As a result, many people find themselves adrift, way off their bearing and many degrees from their true north. This is because they've become too wrapped up in the pressures and humdrum of life, thinking they would eventually get to it at some point. It is often only when things reach crisis point, disillusionment or a feeling of being severely lost that they want to find a compass bearing to regain some direction in their life.

HURDLES: Even once you've gained clarity around your five pillars, I wish it was simply a case of being proactive and taking the required action. However, there are often hurdles to overcome or navigate such as politics, mindset or circumstances. This can take many forms, and the areas I've highlighted are certainly not a definitive list but, rather, an example of what you could come up against.

RESOURCES: The resources column recognizes that there are also supportive tools, techniques and contacts that can help you get there. Again, this isn't a definitive list but serves as a key reminder that, while there may be hurdles to face, there are often resources that people forget to use in gaining access to their true path.

TRUE NORTH: The final column illustrates my belief that once you have identified and aligned your five pillars, you are far more likely to fulfill your potential as you'll more than likely be aligned with your inner calling. The more you are aligned and living true to your pillars, the more likely you'll be in the right position to leverage your true talents and live your true north.

If you are in a hurry and keen to take a short cut, the most effective areas to examine are your five pillars. Once you have gained aspirational clarity here, you can cross-reference against your current position and determine where to act. Here's a quick outline:

- **Personal Aspirations: What do you want out of life?**
  - Tool: Write it out or use the brilliant neuroscience technique *PictureSpark*
  - Video link to PictureSpark: https://www.youtube.com/watch?v=uOi6Qa91cts
- **Business Aspirations: What are your career aspirations?** (Note: This is a blank canvas exercise looking at the possible and the *what if* without being constrained by the present.)
  - Tool: Write it out, record it or use PictureSpark
- **Skillset: What are your innate skills, strengths, and drivers?** (I recommend three key tools to turn a lens on truly understanding what makes you tick and how to align it with your aspirations.)

- **LCP: Discover your leadership signature:** https://leadershipcircle.com/en/ Note: This tool can only be done through a registered practitioner of the LCP
- **Gallup Strengths Finder:** Discover how you align with 34 key traits and how they correlate with the job or career you are currently in. (Pro version online £50)
- **Enneagram iEQ9:** https://www.integrative9.com/enneagram/ This is a phenomenal psychometric tool that dissects your personality and helps illustrate how you operate in the world. (Pro version online £90)

- **Environment: What physical and mental environment would you truly flourish in?**
  - **Tool:** Simply ask yourself what the ideal geographical area and conditions would be that you would like to work in, along with what you would need to flourish mentally too.
- **Values: What are the core values that you inherently live by?**
  - **Tool:** Use a list of 400 values to understand the top ten values you navigate your life by. It is crucial they largely align with the company values of where you work, otherwise you are likely to be in conflict

most of the time which doesn't allow either party to flourish.

- **Tool:** Assess where your mindset sits on the mindset continuum and where you might need a reframe.

This book has been designed and formatted so that you can gain insights, learnings and benefit from each chapter. Therefore, you can freely skip ahead to the chapter that grabs your interest the most. However, you will gain maximum benefit by systematically going through each chapter to build a clear and coherent picture of your own map and where and how you wish to navigate your true path moving forward. I'm truly excited for you to learn how to calibrate your inner compass and carve your path towards your true north like many others before you.

CHAPTER 1

CONTEXT IS EVERYTHING!

Erich's father lost everything at the age of 11. He lost his home, his safety net and his stability. His family had very little money left even for the basics in life; it was an extremely challenging time for all. Erich had to go to a new school and felt embarrassed and ashamed of his circumstances. In fact, it was such an emotional, gut-wrenching event that it scarred and affected Erich to this day.

Pavlov is famous for creating an experiment in the 1900's where he taught dogs to salivate at the sound of a bell. This experiment was based around conditioning and, as humans, we are subject to similar responses depending on the stimuli. In Erich's case, he learned that avoiding risk would likely protect him, but it dropped into his subconscious in the passing of time as he grew up. When I met Erich, he was somewhat frustrated by his risk-averse nature but could not understand why or where it had come from. It wasn't until we explored his childhood that I helped him connect the dots. Once Erich gained clarity around his conditioning, he was able to deconstruct his fear. He realised his brain was on red alert to avoid such catastrophic events even though his circumstances were now completely different. Erich's natural propensity to be safe had guided him to create a vast safety net buffer for any eventualities such as a pension, savings, assets and various other investments. His brain falsely assumed he could be subject to the same catastrophic events at any moment rather than taking a step back and realising he was living in completely different circumstances, unlikely to encounter such drastic fallout.

The mental release of understanding his conditioning has since allowed Erich to break through his fears and insecurities, and to embrace a wonderful new opportunity where he can truly realise his potential and no longer be held back by his subconscious fears.

This story is just one of countless examples where context is *everything*. Over the years, I've realised the more time I take to understand the backdrop, drivers and influences on my client's persona, the more likely I am to be able to shine a light on any blind spots, reveal the elements at play, and ultimately break down the artificial barriers that have been holding them back.

Maybe you suffer from *imposter syndrome*, leadership confidence or communication skills, or you're scared of presentations or sharing your views or perspective in meetings. Whatever it is, it is a unique combination of nature and nurture; your persona along with the experiences you've been subjected to in your childhood and adult life to-date. I suspect the majority of us are experiencing a roadblock or resistance due to key factors at play. My task therefore is to be aware of this and help unravel the root meaning to it all where necessary so that individuals can break free and emerge empowered to reach their full potential whatever their position or role in life.

It is for this reason that I created E3 – a methodology to establish the terrain or position on a life map. It stands for:

> **Explore your Thinking, Examine your Challenges and Execute on a Plan.**

Think of it as, **'Where you've been, where you are and where you want to go?'**

Imagine you were on a road journey or at sea, you'd need to know where you are before you can head in the direction of your choosing– that's why we have signposts and navigational charts. The same goes for your career, but too many clients are intent on racing to *where* they are trying to go before truly understanding their current position.

> **"If I had an hour to solve a problem, I'd spend 55 minutes thinking about the problem and five minutes thinking about the solution."**
>
> ***— Albert Einstein***

It's no different in trying to determine your path forward. Evaluating your position allows you to calibrate where you are and where your lack of clarity/ understanding lies – hence E3 indicating what you need to focus on to achieve focused momentum.

So, how do you orientate your current position? Through clarity! The aim is to truly understand your current position by exploring, analysing and evaluating all the elements at play. When I lead expeditions, I need to truly appreciate the big picture so I can take time to ensure I have the proper clarity and understanding of my competencies, where I want to start and what I need to achieve my objective. Much like a compass works using the magnetic pull of Earth's poles to navigate from a known reference point, our internal compass works in a similar way. Our past, present and future, along with our modus operandi, serve as key bearings on a compass; much like North, East, South and West. And the events in our lives are like positions or trig points on the map.

Just as in the famous fable, "The Tortoise and the Hare," by taking a little extra time to orientate yourself on your life map, you have a far better chance of confidently going in the *right* direction with self-assurance and measured speed rather than haring off in the wrong direction, only having to circumnavigate a route back that may take even longer.

Once I've established a rapport with the individuals I work with and have listened intently to their current circumstances and challenges, I like to hear their life story. There is no right or wrong to this process, but I've learned to be 100% present. It helps that I consider it a true privilege to hear one's story as it is always a fascinating tale; as enjoyable as sitting around a campfire and listening to an adventure tale. The key factor I've found is to put the individual at ease and allow them to talk freely and openly about their childhood, their experiences growing up, their path as young adults and how they have navigated their career path to the present day. Some are happy to launch into this during the first session. Others take a little time before the trust and psychological safety is in place to share their personal experiences, but most clients soon recognize the value in exploring their story as they grapple with their challenges of today.

Haasim grew up in Lebanon in the 1980s. It was a time of great uncertainty amidst a backdrop of civil war. Haasim vividly remembers how each day was a life-threatening event just to get to school. As he described his story, I couldn't help but wonder what impact this had on his conditioning and mindset as a young, vulnerable child.

Has he learnt coping mechanisms to deal with such challenges, or have they adversely affected him to this day?

Fortunately, even when children experience a traumatic event, they don't always develop traumatic stress. Many factors contribute to symptoms, including whether the child has experienced trauma in the past. Various protective factors for the child, such as family and community levels, can reduce the adverse impact of trauma. However, this backdrop would surely factor into Haasim's modus operandi and whether there are subconscious patterns, such as trust or risk, that influence how he navigates the world today.

Arnaud grew up on the idyllic Pacific island of New Caledonia, known for its palm-lined beaches and marine-life-rich lagoon. At the age of 10, his carefree existence was thrown into turmoil as he was uprooted and moved to the hustle and bustle of the city suburbs of Paris. Again, such a severe change of events at such a tender age can have a profound impact on the conditioning of your psyche. Where Arnaud once felt safe and carefree, he was now in an environment which was a lot more challenging and demanded a different set of life skills to survive. The much more hostile school environment meant that Arnaud was far more on guard and became reserved in the face of fresh threats. This experience could either be a learning or a trauma, depending on how it is processed and evaluated at the time.

Lizette is an accomplished and talented doctor. She is a director of her practice and helps numerous patients daily– whether it's a simple cut or sprain to more serious chronic and life-threatening ailments. Her attention-to-detail and accuracy in her diagnosis is a testament to her professionalism. However, some of this drive is rooted in the traumatic experience of losing a patient in her junior doctor years. Although she did everything she could to help the patient, the emotional impact of the patient losing their life scarred her so much that she is now living with PTSD. Lizette's love of being a doctor is also the root of her anxiety and depression. Over time, her mind distorted the expectations of her profession, leading her to believe that she was wholly responsible for each and every patient's life – whatever their condition. This simply isn't true but her PTSD meant she was now living a nightmare, losing sleep, evenings and weekends worrying and overcompensating for every little detail as a physician. She'd lost the ability to balance her responsibility as a physician against the natural course of some inevitable medical conditions.

This is not to say challenging childhoods or certain careers are bad. On the contrary, it teaches us life skills that we may otherwise be immune to, especially if we're born with the proverbial silver spoon in our mouth. If everything is done for you and your every need is catered for, where are the lessons in survival, resilience, fortitude and ingenuity to survive?

It has certainly helped me realise I'm a much more rounded and competent coach today for the turbulent seas I've encountered in creating Jumpstone International.

However, if the conditioning has created a situation later in life that is detrimental to your wellbeing or, worse, preventing you from realizing your true potential, isn't it time to hack into the subconscious and understand how it can be rewired?

Rarely are individuals at either end of the spectrum. They usually fall somewhere between the two. However, each and every one of us has a unique constellation to our lives and I find it fascinating to see how the dots start to emerge – just like constellations in the sky – and reveal what elements are at play in either assisting or preventing people from moving forward in their lives and careers.

This process never ceases to amaze me and my clients as they find clarity around situations they haven't been able to unravel for months, or even years! The Pathfinder approach truly lies at the centre of business, self-help and mindset – like a *Reuleaux Triangle* intersects the three elements - because all these factors come into play as clients clear the fog to their particular circumstances, whether from conditioned experiences, their persona or their current mindset.

My coaching has evolved to swiftly identify a person's current position in business and life. I call it their Present Day GPS. I have honed in on three distinct exercises to triangulate their current position which we will explore in the next chapter.

This is crucial if you are to fully commit to being open to evaluation, vulnerable to understanding and flexible to change for the better.

Compass Calibration: Use E3: Explore your Thinking, Examine your Challenges and Execute a Plan to gain an initial bearing on where you've been, where you are and where you want to go.

CHAPTER 2

CALIBRATING YOUR PRESENT DAY GPS

Nick knew things weren't right but he couldn't put his finger on it so he continued to ignore the disturbance above his head and keep pushing blindly forward. He was so overwhelmed that he kept kicking the proverbial can down the path, hoping the answer would materialize. Twelve months later, he was still in the same spot– only now his relationship, health and job were rapidly unravelling.

Does this sound familiar? It's certainly not unusual. Many individuals are treading water on their problems because that seems easier than swimming miles – especially when you don't know which direction to go to save yourself.

There are a myriad of challenges we might be facing such as financial struggles, business conflicts, family dynamics or even health problems. The list is endless, but it's knowing how to navigate through them, out of them or how to live with them that is key. It may hurt to look in the mirror and admit you're struggling or to find blind spots you weren't aware of but knowledge truly is power. Therefore, the more time we take to understand our circumstances, find clarity around our drivers and conditioning to our responses, the better we can assess what needs to change to move forward.

There are numerous tools, methodologies, and approaches to help individuals find clarity. Tools include psychometric frameworks that analyse your personality, leadership tools that measure your effectiveness and EQ tools that measure your emotional intelligence. Methodologies and theories help explain how you align with the matrix or frameworks that can explain various concepts such as company culture, brand, or communication.

At this stage, it is all too easy to put the horse before the cart and get side-tracked by the intricacies of your job, a challenging dynamic in your life or zoning in on a particular component of your personality. However, the key is to *resist* temptation to go granular and take a step back and take an overarching helicopter view of your life. The Pathfinder Model helps you to do this by evaluating your job situation first, your life position second and your modus operandi third. Once you have gained a snapshot of your current position, you will be ready to examine your five pillars in life so that you can cross-reference your aspirations against your current life position or 'Present Day GPS'.

Trig Point: Many individuals try to blame their circumstances for their shortcomings over themselves. Therefore, they are inclined to jump ship and try elsewhere, only to fall into the same trap and discover that whatever they are trying to avoid will follow them.

The key is to work out if it is the *circumstances* you are in or the way you operate before you can make the right decision to move forward. This isn't easy; it's like looking at a picture or into a mirror too closely. You only gain perspective once you take a step back or, even better, use an external soundboard to help you find the clarity you need.

This may prove to be the answer, but without true clarity around your modus operandi, whatever is proving a barrier or block to your success, is more than likely to follow you to the next role.

Laura is a case in point. Her life was in chaos, and she felt she had way too much on her plate. She believed the answer lay in taking on a new role in a new company. To her dismay, it was the classic jumping out of the frying pan and into the fire. It wasn't until we took a step back together that we discovered her propensity to fill her life was due to the fear of missing out. She also felt she had something to prove as her internal mindset was often saying, "I'm not good enough so I need to prove myself."

As for Nick who we started this chapter with, it was a classic case of Nancy Kline's '*Time to Think*'. We both love hiking so we took on a peak that would take us nearly four hours to summit in the Austrian Alps. On our journey up the mountain, Nick found clarity which he eloquently shared in a LinkedIn post:

> *"Our discussion flowed effortlessly as we walked. Very quickly I find that we are in conversation and not a Q&A. We start to explore my 'purpose.' Are you satisfied with the scores for family, friends, social, etc. Why do you think they are scoring lower than you would like? How could you adjust those results? What would need to change? If you succeeded in making those adjustments, how would it impact you? Your kids? Your extended family, etc. What stops you from making those adjustments? What do you think has prevented you from doing so before now? Red flag 2: in answer to the question 'what would need to change' I always answered with the need to 'sacrifice' a work commitment rather than lead with a family priority.*

I can't tell you exactly where we were on the trail when I was to have an epiphany moment and I won't bore you with trying to explain exactly what that moment of clarity revealed. But what I can tell you is that in an unprovoked moment during the ascent, I had absolute clarity as to my purpose and shock at the realisation of the fact that I had been both blind to it and its ramifications.

It's fair to say that I feel upbeat. I feel a greater sense of satisfaction and perhaps more balanced. I genuinely believe that my family & friends would also note a positive change. I realise that the 'suspension' that was dampening the effects of the irregular wheel of life was in fact my ability to ignore the issues and maybe even avoid dealing with them by focusing more intensely on my work. My workplace performance is better than ever."

You see, in Nick's case, all it took was a step back and a severe jolt from the autopilot he had become accustomed to. With other clients, there may be more subtle factors at play that require a more forensic approach to observe what's out of kilter or what needs to be addressed to identify how and where the dots connect. What I do know is that if you never take time to think, it's unlikely you'll find your true path.

PRESENT DAY GPS:

The fundamental challenge is knowing your own present-day GPS bearing. This is where the Pathfinder Model comes into its own. Once you understand where things are working and where there is friction or confusion, you can address it as you see fit.

The third column represents the current reality. The top segment represents an individual's current job role and everything it entails. The middle *wheel of life* diagram represents the present-day snapshot of their current circumstances by calibrating their position across key areas of life. The bottom segment represents their *modus operandi* and how effectively they are leveraging their talents and interpersonal skills to achieve their goals, objectives, and aspirations.

Your present-day GPS is an amalgamation of everything that has happened to this point and how you have navigated your challenges, setbacks and opportunities to-date with the mindset you have cultivated. An interesting observation at this point is the more mindful and in tune you've been with your aspirations to this point, the closer you're likely to be to your true north. You may align with society's classic perspective of success – high powered job, good salary, nice house, high-spec car etc., but its largely irrelevant if it doesn't align with your definition of success. In fact, quite a few of my clients who have all this are often the ones who feel the most lost in life.

This quote from the movie *Shang-Chi* and the Legend of the Ten Rings says it all:

"If you aim for nothing, you'll hit nothing."

Many executives share that they ended up in their career roles and it evolved and grew from an initial opportunity at the outset of their career. However, if it was in an area that wasn't intrinsically of interest, there is a good chance that the job to-date is a means to an end rather than serving a true intrinsic passion. It's no surprise to me that a global poll conducted by Gallup uncovered that, out of the world's one billion full-time workers, only 15% of people are engaged at work. That means that an astronomical 85% of people are unhappy in their jobs!

While a professional coaching soundboard reveals true insights about their position, it is extremely difficult to unravel exactly what is working and what needs focus and attention. Individuals can take the self-help route along with the trial and error method and they may eventually get there, but it often leads to being further lost in the fog – hence why people give up or promise themselves they'll come back to it another time but rarely do.

So how does an individual know which tool to use, what area to focus on or what areas to explore even if they do engage with a coach?

Each executive coach will either follow a prescribed approach or create their own program that provides a more tailor-made experience. My first step is to triangulate an individual's Present Day GPS position on their current situation. I do this by using three exercises that I've developed to swiftly orientate an individual's position, mindset, and general wellbeing:

True North

No.1 is to determine how close you are to your true north.

For a visual explanation of this tool, please go to the following URL on Jumpstone International's website to see the 2 minute coaching clip **'Orientating your Present Day GPS'**

> URL: https://jumpstoneinternational.com/innercompass-resource/
> Website Resource Password:
> Inner-Compass72!

For this exercise, I ask an individual where they would position their current compass bearing in relation to their true north. I ask "*How close or far away are you?*" There is no scientific calibration to this other than pure gut instinct but, again, it provides a clear visual indication of whether the individual feels they are on track with their life. Some recognize they are close e.g. a NNE bearing which is great, but it still helps them to recognise whether they are on a curve moving towards or away from their true north too. Others suddenly realise they are already way off course by 180°; frustrated and even depressed at the thought of ending up so far in the wrong direction. There is a timeline factor to this exercise, too. *How long have they been going in this direction and what have you done to correct the course?* This initial Present Day GPS positioning is crucial to orientating the client.

Curve of Life

No.2 is to discover where an individual is on their 'Curve of Life.'

For a visual explanation of this tool, please go to the following URL on Jumpstone International's website to see the 2 minute coaching clip **'Where are you on the Curve of Life'**

URL: https://jumpstoneinternational.com/innercompass-resource/
Website Resource Password:
Inner-Compass72!

I keep this deliberately vague as I don't want to condition their response because everyone's perception of success is different. I examine whether they are behind the curve of life, in line with where they should be for their age, experience and knowledge, or ahead of the curve. Their response is often a reflection of the vibe they emanate. If an individual's disposition gives off an aura of being on edge, impatient, frustrated or even angry, I predict they will lie *behind* the curve. If my client is at ease, comfortable in their own skin and in the present, it is often an indication they are where they feel they should be or ahead of the curve. This isn't always the case, but 95% of the time it correlates with their disposition. This exercise alone can open Pandora's box as it is very often the first time a client sees, with clarity, where they are truly positioning themselves in life.

No.3 is to assess their general belief in themselves. I ask the following question:

"Are you good enough but trying to get better?" Or "Are you not good enough and therefore need to get better or prove something?"

It may sound subtle but there is a profound chasm between the two as it often illustrates someone's core mindset right from the word go. I stress to my clients that I make observations, not judgements and, at this stage, while it may be tempting for them to escape, frightened down the rabbit hole. However, evaluating their Present Day GPS empowers them to step away from the fear of the unknown. As they learn about their psyche and where they currently stand, they gain a greater sense of self awareness and begin to feel hopeful about the possibilities for change ahead. After all, knowledge is power!

Sometimes a blank canvas of opportunity is more frightening than liberating, so I've created five key pillars which are instrumental in providing razor-sharp clarity around the key totems in your life. In the next chapter, we will explore how they will allow you to imagine the best possible version of your life so you can cross-reference how well aligned you are against your inner compass. Once you gain this perspective, you can more easily calibrate back against how well your Present Day GPS is meshing for your job, personal time and modus operandi in your everyday life.

Compass Calibration: Use the following three exercises to determine your current position (personal GPS) in your life:

- Calibrate your current position against your True North
- Determine where you on the Curve of Life
- Mindset question. Ask yourself: "Are you good enough or not good enough?"

CHAPTER 3

THE 5 PILLARS TO CLARITY

Gretchen was a chiropractor who enjoyed her job but she could feel a nagging itch that there was something better. Her husband Grant was in a near crisis. He had been a teacher for 22 years and was at the end of his tether. His original love for the job had turned into a daily nightmare of long hours, admin grind and little time to focus on the areas of teaching that had originally inspired him. He wanted out, but what could he do? He felt totally trapped. He often considered retraining, but indecision held him back along with his advancing years. "It's too late, isn't it?" he wondered. He was convinced it would take too long, a time and investment they could ill afford, and he wasn't even sure what he'd retrain in if given the opportunity.

Diana thought she knew what her career aspirations were but how on earth were they going to dovetail into having children and travelling the world, let alone having the free time to run a business? Her rational brain, or prefrontal cortex, was telling her to start a business, while her subconscious was telling her she needed to find security in her physiological and safety needs first (Maslow's hierarchy of needs). She was caught in a start-stop pattern for months not knowing why one part of her was motivated and the other part was apathetic.

The personal and business aspiration pillars revealed the answer for both these examples which I explain below. PictureSpark – a powerful neuroscience technique worked its wonders again in finding the clarity they needed. Gretchen and Grant both discovered a joint venture they both felt inspired by and could reinvigorate their joy for life.

I feel my own story is worth sharing too. I was worn out from my daily 1.5 hour commute from York to Hull. In fact, I was so tired, I often had to stop on the way home and have a power nap to stop myself from falling asleep at the wheel. In my early forties with two young kids, no savings, I was living month-to-month and still renting, despite having a senior role in higher education. I knew I'd chased experiences rather than the 'green back' as my friend called it, but I'd always been conscientious and worked hard.

So, why couldn't I get ahead? I was earning over £45,000 but still felt like I was going backwards. I was disillusioned with the prospect of working in higher education for the rest of my career, but I'd already danced around trying to find my vocation. Yes, there were perks of international travel but with no prospects of increasing my salary to have any measurable effect on my income. So what could I do, where could I go? *How could I change things?*

Seven years later, I am the CEO of my own flourishing company, providing powerful impact for my clients while largely working my chosen hours with enough time to be a fully engaged family man enjoying life with my wife and kids. *How?* Through finding forensic clarity around the 5 pillars in the Leadership Pathfinder Plan.

I created these five pillars to allow an individual to gain true insight into how they envision how they wish to live key areas in their life. I've discovered over my years as an executive coach that too many people are passive or reactive in steering their lives. They are often reacting to subconscious factors that influence their direction in life such as mindset, career carrots, or family expectations without enough clarity around where and what they are trying to achieve in alignment with their aspirations. As a result, many people find themselves adrift, off bearing and many miles from their destination because they became too wrapped up in the pressures and humdrum of life, thinking they would get to it at some point. It is often only when things reach crisis point, disillusionment or a feeling of being lost that people feel compelled to regain a meaningful bearing to their life.

The other problem people often encounter is *confusion*. Their thoughts are often a swirl of aspirations intertwined with guilt. They throw up questions like, Am I asking for too much? Am I fussing? Shouldn't I be grateful for what I have and just get on with it? Look at how my parents and grandparents grafted in life just to give me the basics. Why should I do what I please?

Of course, these thoughts often lead to a state of paralysis or treading water. They know they *want* to move forward but they're confused when it comes to the *how*. So, it makes more sense to just stay put until the answer or solution comes to them. The trouble is that viable solutions rarely fall into your lap unprompted. Another false temptation is a promotion. Yes, it feels good and creates fresh momentum, but often in the wrong direction. The individual is left knowing it doesn't feel right, but hey, at least they made a change! If this is the case, it only takes 6 months or so before the sense of frustration returns often in parallel with greater responsibility and stress.

But what if you could evaluate key areas in your life and have a true sense of knowing you are on track, on the right bearing. What if you had the clarity to know what was working and what needs attention? What if you had the ability to evaluate those areas or blind spots that need focus and attention to enable transformation on the right bearing?

The five Pathfinder pillars have proved themselves to be instrumental in giving my clients that clarity. They are as follows:

Personal Aspirations:	**What do you want out of your personal life?**
Business Aspirations:	**What are your career goals?**
Skillset:	**What are your innate skills, strengths & drivers?**
Environment:	**What physical and mental environment would truly allow you to flourish?**
Values:	**What are the core values you inherently live by?**

Personal and Business Pillars

It is crucial that the first two pillars dovetail rather than create conflict but they are also the hardest to fathom. It's all very well asking a client what they want out of life but many struggle to articulate what that actually means to them. There are obviously various methods and techniques to do this – from drawing pictures, thinking of metaphors, or answering lengthy questionnaires – but by far and above the most effective method I've discovered is the *neuroscience of imagery*.

Back in 2014, when I first started out, one of my clients was struggling to articulate his challenges. I felt frustrated for him as I sensed he had it within him, but he couldn't put his finger on it. I happened to have a box of random images as one of my coaching tools, so I suggested he use imagery to connect with his inner thoughts. It was astounding. My client went from being confused and muted to articulated and animated. Clearly, something phenomenal had just happened, but I couldn't explain the science. It was only a few months later that I discovered the neuroscience and it has since become a cornerstone of the coaching tools I use today.

One's intuition, gut instinct, or sixth sense are all forms of subconscious. It is so powerful because it is the hard drive or guidance system of our brains. It is our true powerhouse, storing the whole gamut of our lives – from our emotions and beliefs to our memories and experiences. Incredibly, neuroscience is revealing that what we think are sound, conscious decisions are in fact revelations brought up from deep down in our subconscious brain. Therefore, our deliberation over problems, challenges and conundrums isn't working out the problem at all. It is more akin to treading water until our two brains connect and provide a communication channel to the clarity from our subconscious!

The 'Genius of PictureSpark' allows us to bypass this often lengthy deliberation by tapping into our natural database of knowledge - thereby allowing us to discover what makes us and our businesses tick. So, whether we need a trusted soundboard to our thinking, a strategic steer or creative insight, the Genius of PictureSpark allows us to find clarity and direction to solve an infinite number of challenges - whether they are personal, business or random in nature.

This technique is not particularly new; in fact, coaches have been using imagery for some time to help clients articulate a thought, meaning or interpretation through an image. But it has been haphazard at best, and often results in *more* confusion.

However, it has proved so powerful in helping clients pinpoint what they previously couldn't put their finger on, that I honed and developed this technique until there was a coherent and effective framework to consistently deliver results. This has evolved to become *PictureSpark*.

How does PictureSpark work?

The Genius of PictureSpark is a swift but very effective shortcut to the subconscious. It consists of 150 random photographic images that provide a range of subjects, scenarios and perspectives, naturally provoking different interpretations depending on the individual looking at them.

Please refer to the web link below to see a video explanation of the '**Genius of PictureSpark**'

URL: https://jumpstoneinternational.com/innercompass-resource/
Website Resource Password:
Inner-Compass72!

Once the individual (or group) has determined a challenge to explore such as, "what do I want to achieve in my career?", "What are the top five challenges we're currently grappling with in the business?" or "What are the top 5 unique selling propositions of our brand?", they stop trying to think about it and, instead, allow their eyes to act as a window to their subconscious. As their eyes scan the cards, the subconscious brain is immediately 'fired' and starts searching and connecting with images that resonate with the challenge or question.

The subconscious creates an emotional pull akin to the gut instinct we've all felt, telling us which card or cards to pick. The process of picking the cards often takes less than a a few minutes. The individual then selects the images they have chosen and allows *The Genius of Picture Spark* to flow as the channel between the subconscious and conscious brains connect, bringing to the surface clarity on the problem.

Clients often end up with several images, representing the puzzle pieces of the bigger picture. They can then see how they all correlate to provide a razor-sharp lens to their problem or challenge. Clients are astounded at the speed and clarity they find on problems, challenges and issues that they've previously spent days, weeks or months going around and around in circles, feeling lost and confused. If you would like to read about the neuroscience of imagery further, then I recommend an amazing book called, '*Perception and Imaging*' by John Suler and Richard Zakia. They explain in-depth how and why the neuroscience of imagery is not a gimmick and why it provides such powerful and insightful results.

Many of my clients have often said things like, '*I've tried countless times to work out what I want in life but never found the answer. I get hints here and there, but I can't ever find a way to focus or channel the ideas into a clear path.*' They've then tried PictureSpark and have been amazed at the clarity and accuracy they've found within a session.

Skills Pillar

The next pillar is the Skills Pillar. It is crucial to know what you bring to the table if you are going to leverage it successfully. However, there are so many psychometric tools out there, e.g. Myers Briggs (MBTI), Thunderbird, the Neethling Brain Instrument (NBI™), Belbin, Disc to Emotional Intelligence, Intercultural Development Inventory® (IDI®), you could spend weeks analysing your personality in micro detail and still not be clear on what you're meant to do with them. I've taken and worked with many of these tools, but I've found the unique combination of three will offer the insight needed to understand your leadership, your strengths and your personality, and how they dovetail into your career, life and modus operandi.

1. Leadership Circle Profile

The Leadership Circle Profile™ (LCP) is a true breakthrough among 360-degree profiles. It is the only instrument that measures the two primary leadership domains (creative competencies and reactive tendencies) and integrates this information for immediate opportunities for leadership development. It provides an integrated lens of a leader's unique operating system and helps evaluate their overall effectiveness. It interprets their internal assumptions (beliefs) that run behavior in both domains and illustrates how the inner world of thought translates into either a productive or unproductive style of leadership. Unlike most profiles that take hours to interpret, the LCP makes it easily accessible while increasing awareness to provide the individual the opportunity for tangible change in behaviour.

In most organisations, this treasure trove of information remains buried, but the data in the LCP reveals itself in seconds - putting leaders in touch with what is working, what is not, and why!

2. Gallup Clifton Strengths

Many of my clients wonder who they truly are and what makes them unique.

The CliftonStrengths Assessment provides clarity to answer those questions. It calibrates the intensity of a person's talents across 34 traits, providing a unique profile.

The true value in Gallup's model is their philosophy against the grain of our education system. Most people are taught to work on their weaknesses; to *fix* them. But instead, Gallup believes they should be learning how their strengths can overshadow their weaker areas. Being well-rounded doesn't necessarily lead to higher performance. You can achieve the highest levels of success only when you stop trying to be a little bit good at everything and instead hone what you are naturally best at.

In other words: Focus less on being well-rounded and more on becoming better at what you're already great at. Discovering your strengths is just the start; applying and *investing* in them sparks real change. This tool provides a valuable backdrop to the coaching process of understanding your modus operandi and how you can apply them, empowering you to realise your full potential.

3. ieQ9 Enneagram

The Integrative Enneagram offers an unparalleled depth of insight into enneagram types, personality, motivation, and self-limiting beliefs, creating the potential for accelerated, integrative and sustainable development in individuals, teams or organisations.

This tool is so accurate that I often tell my clients it's like a combination of someone who knows me better than my parents and has cut me in half and read my DNA.

The iEQ9 Enneagram's adaptive, intelligent questionnaires integrate the art and science of self-discovery and transformation with intelligent, cutting-edge technology.

As well as the most comprehensive Enneagram profile (including 27 Subtypes, Wings and Levels of Integration) their comprehensive reports also reflect Six Dimensions of Stress and Strain, centres of expression (thinking, feeling and action) and the interpersonal or team implications for communication and conflict, leadership and decision-making and team behaviour.

Their practical and accessible format allows for self-driven learning and intentional, powerful action and development strategies. All reports offer customized advice and development paths for each subtype, which can be applied immediately. Again, this report allows the coaching dynamic to explore the findings in context and how it relates to their current GPS position, as well as how it can be leveraged to move the needle towards their inner compass.

Once my clients have the results of all three tools, they can cross-reference back across to their current GPS position and clearly see how aligned they are with their current role, wheel of life, and modus operandi in context to their conditioning and career path.

Environment Pillar

The fourth pillar is the environment. In essence, it's important to know what mental and physical environment you need to truly flourish. If you took a step back to observe the last 150 years, it would illustrate rapid change. Despite this, we've generally had a blueprint to the workplace that people could adapt to.

However, COVID-19 has been unprecedented in creating monumental challenges, making us feel like lab rats in our own laboratory. We've been forced to find out what works for us under dynamic circumstances such as working from home (WFH), lockdowns, evolving business terrain, fluctuating business dynamics, online conference fatigue, clash of parental demands, financial strain, and social unease as well as psychological stress and repetitive strain injuries.

In fact, COVID-19 has had such a profound impact on the workplace that it has created a seismic shift in how businesses operate. No generalized resilience initiative or crisis communication session could have fully prepared organizations for today's new reality, and leaders have had no training for this pandemic scenario; they are in the dark as to how to support themselves, let alone their staff in how to navigate these pressures.

I heard recently that it has either made us 'a hunk, a chunk, or a drunk!' Joking apart, it's not far off as some of us have flourished under COVID, loving the opportunity to work from home, avoiding the commute, feeling more integrated with the family, and finding balance for our lives. Others have unfortunately ended up with serious mental side effects due to living in a pressure cooker with no release valve. In fact, they're already talking about post-COVID being the new mental health crisis which is also creating a reaction in the general workforce provoking what the press have dubbed 'The Great Resignation'.

Therefore, it's clear to see why the environment pillar is a crucial part of the framework. I haven't developed or recommended a specific tool for this pillar, but it is important to give yourself time and headspace to write down and reflect on your needs. The key is to go to the white box again and not be constrained by any parameters or circumstances in asking what mental and physical environment you would truly flourish in. Too many individuals make the mistake of saying, "I can't do that because my partner wouldn't live there, or I don't have the money, or my job wouldn't allow it." Remember, you are envisioning where *you would like* to live and work– don't let *anything* hold you back at this stage.

This COVID life juncture is a perfect opportunity to seriously evaluate your environment pillar. The workplace is rapidly evolving to create dynamic opportunities to fit the fresh demands of workers who have been forced to calibrate their needs. Those who are proactive in assessing their needs are ideally placed to take advantage and provide themselves the best chance to flourish under this pillar.

The beauty of this exercise is that it allows you to dream again. Some clients have said it proved to be such a liberating exercise, it reminded them of their carefree imagination from their childhood days.

Values Pillar

The values pillar examines your deep-rooted moral compass. Your values reflect your sense of right and wrong or what "ought" to be. They are formed by the confluence of our personal experiences and the particular culture we are entwined in. Values are also imposed from our family in childhood and reinforced through culture and life experiences. They dictate the choices we make and determine the direction that our lives take. Our values influence our decisions and strongly correlate to our wheel of life and how we engage in the world around us.

Despite this importance, few people consider evaluating and choosing their values. Instead, they simply adopt the values of their parents and the dominant values of society. Likely, the values you internalized as a child have remained with you through adulthood. Unfortunately, these values may not be serving you and may even be causing internal conflict in your subconscious. You are aware of it but can't make sense of it, especially if you're living along a path that you instinctively know is going in the *wrong* direction.

My clients often forget the importance of values and remark it makes sense when I explain that they are not triggered by what appears to be the cause on the surface i.e., a frustrating project, a disagreeable colleague, or company protocol, but whether it conflicts with their values and belief system. The other fascinating thing that is obvious but often forgotten is that each and every one of us has a unique value system, much like a fingerprint. We mistakenly think others must live by a similar value system – particularly if we are of the same culture – but the unique combination of factors may trigger one individual while another might simply shrug their shoulders.

Meetings are an ideal place to witness this phenomenon. One individual might be incredulous while everyone around them seems indifferent to the information or fact that's just been shared. This is your value system kicking in right there and, if you are rooted in it, you are unlikely to let go, even if others want to move on or dismiss its importance.

The key point here is that our value system is connected to our health and wellbeing, and the extent to which we are either living in harmony or in conflict is determined by how much we are living aligned to our inner compass. This exercise allows you to be more aware and cognisant of the values system you live by and whether it aligns with your job role, your life, and your modus operandi.

So, how do you identify your value system? The most effective method I have found to-date is to use 250 values alphabetically ordered from A to Z, starting with Acceptance and finishing in Zeal. The reason for this is that the greater number of words you use, the more likely you are to zero in on the exact word that reflects what your value. An example of a string of words could be:

Adventure – Curiosity – Discovery – Exploration – Spontaneity – Variety

These words are all similar but have a subtle nuance which all mean something slightly different. By comparing and asking which one reflects your true feelings, you can home in on the word that truly aligns with your value.

Discovering what top 5 to 10 values we live by is often a revelation to my clients. It is a simple but effective exercise to do. You simply take the comprehensive list of up to 250 values and tick off the ones that resonate with you. I ask my clients to repeat the exercise until they can distil it down to their top 10. What you are left with is a distinct list of values that illustrate your moral fibre.

Summary

Once you have gone through each pillar, you will have obtained much greater clarity across all five pillars. This allows you to make a full assessment against your Present Day GPS. Many clients feel a combination of overwhelm and excitement as they start to gain real clarity for the first time in a long time but are apprehensive as they still don't know which direction to align with their inner compass to generate forward momentum to their true north. In the next chapter will we explore how you can orientate your inner compass.

Compass Calibration: By examining each of these pillars in detail, you will be able to focus the lens to find true clarity in finding your inner compass bearing for renewed direction in your life:

- **Personal Aspirations: What do you want out of life?**
  - Tool: PictureSpark or write it out
  - Video link to PictureSpark: https://www.youtube.com/watch?v=uOi6Qa91cts
- **Business Aspirations: What are your career aspirations?** (Note: This is a blank canvas exercise, looking at the possible and the 'what if's' without being constrained by the present.)
  - Tool: PictureSpark or write it out
- **Skillset: What are innate skills, strengths, and drivers?** (I recommend three key tools to turn a lens on truly understanding what makes you tick and how to align it with your aspirations.)
  - **LCP: Discover your leadership signature:** https://leadershipcircle.com/en/ (This tool can only be done through

Jumpstone International or another practitioner of the LCP.)

- ❍ **Gallup StrengthsFinder:** Discover how you align with 34 key traits and how they correlate with the job or career you are currently in.
- ❍ **Enneagram iEQ9:** https://www.integrative9.com/enneagram/ (Note: this is a phenomenal psychometric tool that dissects your personality and helps illustrate how you operate in the world.

- **Environment: What physical and mental environment would you truly flourish?**
  - ❍ **Tool:** Simply ask yourself what the ideal geographical area and conditions would be ideal for you to work in, and what conditions i.e. office hours, company culture, colleagues, etc would allow you to flourish mentally.
- **Values: What are the core values that you inherently live by?**
  - ❍ **Tool:** Use the list to understand what values you navigate your life by. It is crucial they largely align with the company values of where you work, otherwise you are likely

to be in conflict most of the time which won't allow either party to flourish.

- **Tool:** Assess where your mindset sits on the mindset continuum and where you might need a reframe.

CHAPTER 4

ORIENTING YOUR INNER COMPASS

Tammy was miserable. As CFO of an oil and gas company, she knew she was a valuable asset doing an important job– but why was everyday a struggle? She liked her team, she was happy where she lived, and she was confident in her role. So, what was it that was dragging her down?

When I first met Tammy, I was immediately impressed by her professionalism and work ethic and instinctively knew she was likely to be an asset wherever she worked. It fascinated me why things weren't aligning.

I took the usual approach of E3: Explore your Thinking, Examine your Challenges and Execute on a Plan. But it still didn't reveal the core of Tammy's unhappiness. I then decided to explore the various pillars. Both her personal and business pillars were well-aligned and her skillset was being maxed out, but the bottom two pillars of Environment and Values revealed all. "What environment would you flourish in?" I asked her. "Well, I'd love a naturally lit room with the sun able to stream in. I'd like to be able to open the windows and smell and taste the fresh air. I'd like my office to be mine but have open access for my staff to come and go; I like to be fully engaged with the team."

"So, where do you work currently?" I asked. "In the basement." Naturally, the look on her face said it all when she realised the answer to her physical environment had been staring her in the face all along. However, this still wasn't it. Tammy's desired mental environment - which is shaped by both our mindset and the company culture - didn't align with Tammy's vision. She realised that, while she respected most of the board, they didn't align with her values. The last pillar pulled everything into perspective.

Remember, whether we realise it or not, these values shape our lives daily and often govern how we navigate work and life. When we are triggered, it is often because our values are being compromised or someone says or does something in direct conflict with how we believe we should live our lives. This exercise was a revelation for Tammy as she soon discovered that the company environment she was working in was 90% or more in direct conflict with her values.

In most cases, it is a combination of factors, but the environment and values pillars were *so* out of kilter, it pretty much confirmed what Tammy's gut had been saying for over a year: she needed to move on!

This is just one example, but for everyone, the set of circumstances is different. The key is in connecting the dots to determine what factors are at play - rather like finding constellations from the stars. Once you've gained clarity on where you stand on each of your pillars, you're able to cross-reference them against your present day GPS. What becomes immediately obvious is where it's working, but more importantly, where there is conflict, pain, or friction and whether they are due to the external circumstances you are operating within versus your modus operandi.

The key question to ask is:

"Is it working for you?"

Be honest. If it is, great! If it isn't, ask yourself, "What do I need to learn, change, or improve upon?"

In Tammy's case, she knew there were professional development areas she could work on, but she also knew that whatever she did to improve herself, she was still in the wrong company culture to meet her underlying values.

The professional soundboard is key at this stage because we are often too close to see what's at play or where we are constricted by our conditioning. It is vital that we step back at this point to determine whether it is *external* to you or *because* of you.

To help orientate your *inner compass* further, it is vital to understand your motivations.

Motivation

Motivation is the internal force or desire to act towards a goal. Whether we define it as a drive or a need, it is influenced by the self or our environment and the amount and persistence of effort to act is dependent on the level of will or desire to succeed.

The psychological needs can be driven by the desire for mastery, independence, or greater understanding. It may also be other factors such as the need for achievement, power, closure, meaning, or self-esteem.

Our environment and social context also play a significant role and helps explain four key types of motivation at play:

	Action	**Non Action**
External	EXTRINSIC	IDENTIFIED
Internal	INTRINSIC	INTROJECTED

Action Oriented Motivation

Extrinsic Motivation

Extrinsic motivation comes from outside of us. We do it because we are impelled to; for example, because we are told to by someone who has power over us. Many company motivation systems work on the principle of extrinsic rewards, where people are employed and then commanded. Whilst this is effective for simple activities, it is less useful when you want a person to be self-driven.

Intrinsic Motivation

Intrinsic motivation is done for internal reasons; for example, to align with values or simply for the pure pleasure of doing something. In work, people are intrinsically motivated by working for an inspiring leader or in areas where they have a personal intrinsic interest.

Non-Action Oriented Motivation

Identified Motivation

Identified motivation is pointed out by someone else where you agree something needs doing but you have not yet decided to do anything about it. This is often because of confusion, fear or clash of commitments where other needs win out. An example could be to learn a new skill for the role or to learn a language.

Introjected Motivation

Introjected motivation is an intrinsic motivation, so it still *comes from within but nothing is currently being done about it*. The distinctive aspect of this is that in not being done, the person feels a level of tension often felt as guilt. An example could be wanting to lose weight or write a book but not doing anything about it.

Once I have shared the deeper principles of motivation with my clients, I often suggest they break down and list all their daily work and personal commitments. They then simply tick which commitments fall under the extrinsic or intrinsic column. It very quickly illustrates if they are largely driven by extrinsic factors or if they have a balance with their intrinsic motivations. It's no surprise that clients whose job role better aligns with their intrinsic desires have greater job satisfaction and contentment in their careers.

The key observation I share with people is that companies often gravitate to the extrinsic needs of the business (understandable but misguided) rather than first explore the intrinsic motivations of their employees. If more leaders, managers, and businesses incorporated this into their monthly and annual KPI and performance reviews, it would help align the motivations of both sides. If the company is blinded or unwilling to do this, then the onus falls on the individual to be proactive in steering opportunities more aligned to their intrinsic motivations. It's no surprise that the most powerful motivational factor is intrinsic and this is where goals, objectives, and KPIs will most likely be achieved.

It is also important to be aware of motivational saboteurs that may be hindering your progress. This is where the Wheel of Life can help, first created by Paul J. Meyer.

Wheel of Life

The Wheel of Life exercise is an established coaching tool and is so effective that it is an essential component in Jumpstone's Pathfinder Model. It helps you consider each area of your life in turn and assess what's off balance to identify areas that need more attention. It is called the "Wheel of Life" because each area of your life is mapped onto a circle, like the spokes of a wheel. The core represents zero and the outside edge a maximum score of ten. The exercise simply asks you to rate your position on a scale of zero to ten for each of the headings such as career, money, health, relationships, etc., and you end up creating a fragmented pizza as you score each segment.

It is not unusual for my more alpha male clients to squirm or resist such an exercise as they often consider it too "touchy feely," but I often find they are the ones who need clarity the most. The Wheel of Life is powerful because it gives you a vivid illustration of your current position in life versus where you'd like to be.

Once you visually see the positions on the various axis, you can no longer escape the reality that's been sitting in the fog above your head any longer. In fact you feel compelled to act on areas that you have been proverbially kicking down the road. The beauty of this simple but effective model means you can go granular on a topic that scores particularly low. For example, if you scored 2 out of 10 for health, you might wish to do a new wheel looking at all the components of health such as weight, nutrition, exercise, free time, mental well-being, etc. This allows you to home in and pinpoint exactly what area in your life is suffering or being ignored, allowing you to be much more aware of what areas need addressing and require action.

A final exercise I do with my clients is to calibrate where they would like to be to determine the biggest gaps in their wheel. It may be that you scored 3 on money and want to get to be a 5 whereas you might score 3 on family and would rather be at 9. Therefore, the family needs greater attention.

The final area on the Present Day GPS column is your modus operandi. This is your manner and habits of working, otherwise known as your interpersonal skills. This is crucial to examine and understand so you can determine if it is your persona and disposition at play or external factors that can explain your barriers or current compass bearing pointing in the wrong direction. This deserves its own chapter which we will examine in Chapter 5 so you can learn about tangible coaching tools and methodologies to accurately calibrate your skills, strengths, and innate talents.

Compass Calibration: Evaluate the following three distinct GPS trig points to determine how well your life is currently aligned and operating for you:

Career profile: How well aligned are you with what you instinctively know should be a fit for your career? Ask yourself "Is it working for you?" and you dovetailing your extrinsic and intrinsic motivations?

Wheel of Life: What areas do you need to address in your current life right now? Is it in harmony or in conflict?

Modus operandi: Ask yourself "How well are you leveraging your interpersonal skills in life?" Do you have blind spots, are you distorting them and what aspects do you need to improve upon?

CHAPTER 5

UNDERSTANDING YOUR MODUS OPERANDI

What do we mean by 'modus operandi'? Essentially, it's how we tick or, as the dictionary puts it, "a particular way or method of doing something, especially one that is characteristic or well-established." *Why should that matter?*

Well, the way we operate is a unique combination of nature versus nurture. It is what is inherent in our personality and what we have learnt, observed or mimicked through conditioning as we've grown up. Many individuals have developed hang-ups, fears or blind spots but can't understand where or *how* they were formed.

When I explore a client's modus operandi with them, I'm initially curious what they have to say. I start with a thorough questionnaire that explores key areas of their life, their thinking, and their positions on a number of traits. This gives me a steer as to their current Present Day GPS and where their pain points lie. I then dig in using various tools to see how all the elements interact.

Kristie is a phenomenal doctor whose key strength is effective communication. Her patients say it, her colleagues share it and her family knows it– so why does she think she's no good at it? When I first met her, she even told me outright, "I'm no good at communicating!" She shared that she feels anxious and gets sweaty palms before she needs to onboard a new staff member, and she rarely gets a good night's sleep before presentation days. How can this be when all the evidence before her says otherwise? Her Leadership Circle Profile results even says she is a *phenomenal* communicator.

When I shared this evidence, she simply shrugged her shoulders in self-denial and said, "I'm not *that* good – it's probably because I prepare so much." I responded with a thought-provoking question I've learnt through NLP training:

"When did you decide this?"

"Mmmm?," Kristie murmured and sat back mulling over the direct question as she cradled her face in bemusement. Suddenly, she perked up, cocked her head, and said with fresh clarity, "It was third grade! We had to do a book report on a famous person. I love sports and one of the options was Babe Ruth. I had just received a book about Babe Didrikson, and I just figured they were the same person. It wasn't until I went to give the oral presentation of my report that I realised my mistake. I was ridiculed by everyone, even my teacher...things were different in the late 70s!"

I then asked Kristie how that made her feel. "Just terrible," she responded. "I wanted the floor to swallow me up! It was so demoralizing and humiliating. However, the book about Babe Didrikson was extremely inspiring and impactful, so I guess I had the right book after all!"

It might not seem like a big deal today but that experience on a young and impressionable mind was a traumatic, scarring event; enough to influence a conditioned response to Kristie's thinking around her ability to present. Unfortunately, this had likely sunk into her subconscious, carried through into adulthood, becoming her internal mantra ever since. This realisation was both cathartic and emotionally wrenching to discover... *but it's not unusual.*

In fact, most of us have blind spots to varying degrees that are influencing and affecting our modus operandi, daily. I have numerous examples where I've been able to unearth the source of the fears to explain neurosis, doubts or insecurities which are holding back otherwise very capable individuals.

So, what tools do I recommend to help find clarity and direction to these distortions?

The first one I often use, and a favourite of mine, is the risk model. I devised it after working with Libby King – a CEO of an accounting firm in Austin - who couldn't understand some of her team's aversion to risk. She knew she wanted them to be bolder, but it was like a hidden force was preventing them from overcoming their fears.

Risk Model

The *risk model* is made up of three concentric circular zones. The inner one is the comfort zone, the middle one is the stretch zone and the outer one is the risk zone. Anything outside the risk zone is an extreme or spontaneous uncalculated risk. All of us have a natural position on the model. You may slightly differ over the years, but people are generally the same whatever age or stage of their career. It works like so: wherever you sit on the model, I've discovered most people can maneuver one zone in or one zone out from the sweet spot. The more you move inwards, the more comfortable or bored you are with the task at hand. The more you move outwards, the more uncomfortable, pressured and overwhelmed you become. If you go beyond one zone inwards, you'll probably procrastinate on things because you've done it a hundred times before or you're too bored thinking about it, so you find something more stimulating to do wherever there's the opportunity. If you go beyond one zone on your outer edge, you'll probably procrastinate due to fear, doubt, and overwhelm.

The key discovery is that everyone is different, so it gets interesting when clients discover they are at opposite ends to either their boss, peers, or direct reports. It helps explain why projects may stall or stagnate, or why people are finding excuses not to have tackled the project they were asked to start three weeks ago!

Mindset

Mindset was uniquely coined by the now world-renowned Stanford University psychologist, Carol Dweck, in her decades of research on how effectively the brain tunes into achievement and success.

In a fixed mindset, people believe their basic qualities, like their intelligence or talent, are simply fixed traits. They stay in the now, believing what they have is what they've got to play with, rather than considering the opportunity to *develop* them.

They also believe that talent alone creates success—without effort. This is clearly wrong.

In a growth mindset, people believe that their most basic abilities can be developed through motivation, focus and hard work—brains and talent are just the starting point. This view lends itself to learning and a resilience that is essential for continued growth and accomplishment. Virtually all successful people have these qualities.

Teaching a growth mindset creates motivation and productivity in the worlds of business, education, and sports. It enhances relationships and, the more individuals learn about mindset, the more they realise they can have a far greater proactive effect on their lives.

James Anderson has built on Dweck's work by effectively illustrating that rather than being at either end of the spectrum of fixed v growth, the reality is that we lie somewhere between the two on a continuum. This also depends on the particular topic at hand such as how you face challenges, tackle effort or handle mistakes. Anderson's tool is superb at dissecting and evaluating your approach to different key areas and where you may benefit by focusing and learning new behaviours to adopting a more effective growth mindset.

I also like to share what I've coined the *Einstein Effect*. I quiz my clients, asking them: if you were to ask Einstein how much he knew about the universe, what would his response be? They often say 2 or 3%. I then ask them what percentage the average person would award Einstein. They often respond with 90%.

This simple but effective exercise illustrates how we distort our own expertise. I've often found the more you scratch the surface of a topic, the more you realise you don't know– and it's the same with most people. So, even though we're adding to our knowledge and experiences, we score ourselves less and less until we end up with a large distortion to how others perceive us. It's good to be humble but it doesn't help if we shun or reject recognition from others. In fact, this can sometimes become an irritation to those who are trying to compliment you, especially if you continually bat it away saying, "ahhh, it's nothing."

Binary Extremes

Our personality, culture identity, and values all play a part in how we approach various situations in life. However, it gradually becomes our default to the point where it becomes second nature to how we act, behave, and respond. This exercise was introduced to me by a brilliant NLP Master practitioner based in Australia, Reg Malhotra; which had a profound impact on my own life. This exercise is superb at allowing you to take a step back and identify where you may have a particular leaning in one direction over the opposite approach.

The exercise works by taking a look at a pair of words on a scale of 1 to 10, increasing from the centre. Imagine a car dashboard with the needle pivot below zero. You then consider where the needle sits to best represent your default position. You then circle the number to pinpoint your position. If it's too hard to decide, you probably have balance between the two extremes, so you'll be scoring 0 in the exact middle or just slightly to either side on a 1 or 2. If you are scoring 4 or 5 then you have a leaning, but it acts more as a preference rather than a stance. If you score 7 or above on either side, you are probably entrenched in that position. This obviously brings its strengths, but the magic of this exercise is in realizing that you are probably missing the gifts of the opposite side. There are well over 40 pairs of words for the exercise, and you can even add more if there are pairs of words you wish to examine.

You can try it here with a few examples:

FUN										**SERIOUS**									
10	9	8	7	6	5	4	3	2	1	1	2	3	4	5	6	7	8	9	10

BOLD and WELL PRESENTED										**UNDERSTATED**									
10	9	8	7	6	5	4	3	2	1	1	2	3	4	5	6	7	8	9	10

LOGIC										**INTUITION**									
10	9	8	7	6	5	4	3	2	1	1	2	3	4	5	6	7	8	9	10

If you are repelling the opposite side, then you are more than likely missing the gift in your life in what the other side could offer. It takes a moment to get your head around this, but it truly works. I've worked with numerous individuals who have had epiphanies in realising their entrenched position was the cause of friction in their life due to repelling the opposite trait.

Brad is the marketer of a financial advisory consultancy; they deal with high-net-worth individuals and couples who want to wisely invest their hard-earned income. They attract plenty of clients, but their biggest friction point was clients sitting on the fence for a couple of weeks before deciding to go with a different company. Brad scored 9 in understated, and was very proud of it. When I asked him what he saw in 'Bold and Well-Presented', he flinched and said he pictured someone being arrogant, flashy, and in your face. I said, "I get that, but what's the *gift* in that trait?" After a slow start, he rattled off possible gifts:

- Engaging and energetic
- Professional and attentive
- Ready with responses
- Confident and assured in providing the services
- Diligent and more passionate about their promise

Once Brad got into his stride, a realisation broke across his face. He immediately saw what was lacking in his client-facing approach. I'm delighted to report his business took a positive upturn as he learned to lean into his extreme opposite.

This doesn't mean you must change your personality and become the opposite of what you gravitate to – this would sabotage your authenticity. The key is to move from repelling to *leaning into* the opposite trait. In my own example, I discovered having a little more chutzpah or bravado around marketing my executive coaching offering is no bad thing and is actually what clients are probably seeking i.e., greater self-conviction and confidence in my business offering!

The next area that is crucial to grasp is the ability to communicate effectively. It is vital that you examine your proficiency in this area and consider where there could be room for improvement.

Communication Formula

Communication sounds simple on the surface: a simple exchange of information from one person to another. However, I've lost count of how many times a client has said the *one* thing their company needs to work on is *communication*.

We all yearn to be heard. Especially by those who matter most to us—family, friends, co-workers, managers, and acquaintances. It is a fundamental need. Yet, all too often, true communication with others fails. So, what is it about communication that is so difficult?

Why are individuals and companies typically so bad at communicating?

Well, first off, everybody has their own way of communicating. It is influenced by their upbringing, their cultural background, gender, temperament, and more. Secondly, we all interpret things differently, too. In NLP terms, it examines how we receive information that comes from the outside world, how we process it, and how it influences the way we communicate and respond to others.

In fact, it is mind-blowing when you consider every exchange we ever have is unique to us. The same thing may be said by a presenter to a room of 500 people. There will be 500 interpretations of the information that was just shared! For that reason, we may say one thing but the other person hears and interprets something completely different. Misunderstandings inevitably lead to frustration and problems.

Thirdly, our intention may be different to the outcome. We may inadvertently sound rude or speak unkindly, disrespectfully, and demeaning either intentionally or unintentionally. This may cause hurt feelings and create mistrust, making the other person react defensively. Of course, that only exacerbates the situation. At that point, true communication may become utterly impractical. Sometimes we may have a difficult time understanding another's feelings, needs and habits. Without learning humility, patience, and transparent communication, the connection we are aiming for can be slowly eroded rather than improved.

So, what can we do to get ourselves back on the right path, both as individuals and as companies, to improve our communication skills?

- A candid self-examination
- Use a communication formula
- Understand where we sit on cultural orientations
- Consider what other communication barriers could be at play

Our personal communication style is reflected by what words we use, which methods we choose to transmit them, and the tone and body language particular to us.

We often forget that while we may observe others all day, we rarely do it to ourselves. Therefore, take a good look at your own way of communicating—your preferences, style, and expression—it can be one of the most important things you can do to improve communication with others. When there is a communication obstacle and you can't seem to connect, don't immediately think that it is the fault of the recipient. It can very well be that your own communication style is the cause for friction.

Try asking yourself these questions:

- Do I tend to waffle on without getting really to the point?
- Do I sound relaxed or in a hurry? Irritated or friendly?
- Am I talking more than listening?
- Do I interrupt, pull faces, or roll my eyes?
- Do I lack eye contact or focus?
- Am I 100% engaged with whom I'm supposed to be communicating with?
- Am I easily distracted by other things such as people, phones or reading material?
- Is my language helping others to be attentive or tuning me out?
- Does it alienate or encourage conversations and build bridges?
- Am I making others feel heard and respected, or ignored and unappreciated?

The good news is asking these questions can make significant improvements in communicating more effectively. Another great tool to aid in improving your communication skills is the communication formula.

Communication Formula:

Spoken – Heard – Understood – Agreed To – Commitment – Action –Implemented

This seven-step formula is a clever way to break down the interaction going on between two parties, or even a group. It expertly identifies where there could be a breakdown in communication that can explain confusion, resistance, or disagreement. Any interaction starts with either the verbal word or an illustration to convey a message.

The second stage is recognizing whether someone has heard or seen it. This may seem obvious but if you are on Zoom, perhaps the other party is discreetly looking at their phone or computer, only pretending to listen to you. If this is the case, then they've failed at the second hurdle already.

The next step is knowing whether you've been understood. Too many leaders or managers assume that they've been understood when, in reality, the direct report is too scared to say they didn't understand. A good way to ensure you have been understood is to put the onus back on yourself with a question such as, "just to be sure I explained it correctly, could you reiterate what I just shared with you?"

The next step is to consider whether your request or information has been agreed to. Again, it is too easy to assume at this point. If the company structure is very hierarchical, then the message gets lost and misinterpreted like Chinese whispers as it cascades down through the chain of command.

Effective communication calls for more than just an exchange of information. Understanding emotions and intentions behind the information is the main objective. In effect, putting one's thoughts into another person's mind is to help them grasp the full meaning of the intention of what is being said. Respect for the other person has to be the core basis of exchange and must come across in our way of communicating. Only then can we connect, build trust, and make others feel heard and respected. That kind of exchange is gratifying, empowering, and makes us feel appreciated.

So, whether we communicate within the family, at work, or anywhere else, the ultimate benefit of doing it well is improving our relationships with others. This requires us to hear them out as much as for them to hear us—no matter if we agree with each other's point of view or not.

Therefore, communication must remain a two-way street. It cannot and *should not* be a contest of wills. When there is no flow of emotions and no exchange of thoughts back and forth, relationship bridges collapse. This is unfortunate for any type of relationship - but is often *disastrous* for business.

Leadership Signature: A Personal Anecdote

I was rudely awoken at 3 am to tackle an army initiative exercise. I was given 90 minutes to determine the best plan of defence to protect the watershed of a village in a desert oasis from neighbouring warring tribal factions. The information provided included a map and various features of the terrain as well as various timings for walking, yomping, and traveling by horseback. I started to sweat profusely as the panic began to rise, my head exploding trying to work out the mathematical formulas to assess distance and timings. I only had 20 minutes and didn't have any coherent plan to present to the class. I suddenly had an epiphany! I was trying to be like the other officer cadets and work towards what I thought I should be doing. Instead, I sat back and asked myself, "What would I do?" I knew I was creative and felt confident there must be an innovative solution to the problem.

I absorbed the map and terrain and quickly deduced that if I put the camels on the back of a launch boat, I could race across the lake and save the tribe from attack. Once I finished delivering my presentation, the other cadets fell about laughing at the ridiculousness of the plan.

However, the sergeant said, "Hold it there, chaps. It might seem crazy but no one said that it couldn't be done and there is no reason why it wouldn't work. In fact, in all the years we have set this challenge, no one has ever provided such an innovative plan. Well done, Mr. Guiver, but from now on we're going to nickname you the water-skiing camel!"

I recognize I was fortunate in finding a solution at the last minute, but I learnt a very powerful lesson that day. You can only be the best at who you are if you embrace the qualities you've been given. From that day onwards, I knew I had to trust in my signature leadership and not be held hostage to the allure of trying to be something that I'm not because of feelings of inadequacy.

Despite extensive research, leadership continues to remain an elusive and puzzling phenomenon. It is not surprising considering it is an intangible matter, involving humans, not machines and there is no recognised formula that guarantees success as a leader. It is easily discussed but difficult to nail down. There are lists of desirable qualities, but no leader has them *all.*

Although the aim of many of us is to aspire to be the *best* leaders we can be, many of us feel we are inadequate in some way or deficient in certain qualities. This can be exacerbated by our lack of knowledge around what leadership truly is or how it can be leveraged. It doesn't help that many films, our education system and public understanding tend to stereotype the image of strong assertive, self-assured characters, often in a military or business setting that typically lead from the front.

Therefore, many individuals feel compelled to adopt fragmented elements of others they believe to be superior or more effective in their misguided understanding that this will be better than their inferior selves. In fact, the more an individual does this, the more diluted their leadership becomes, often leaving their colleagues lost as to who they are dealing with or what the individual leader stands for.

The truth is there are a myriad of leadership styles out there and all are equally effective, depending on the character that is leveraging the style and the situation at-hand.

I believe it is better to embrace your own leadership, which I've coined your *signature leadership*. The more you can step into the skin of who you are and what you have to offer, the more you can leverage your style with confidence. You can always lean into the elements of *other* leadership styles but don't directly copy what others are doing.

The key is to learn from your heroes or the leaders you admire but integrate it into your own style.

If you observe the likes of famous leaders such as Muhammed Ali, The Dalai Lama, Ernest Shackleton,

Elon Musk, or Steve Jobs, they all have one distinct trait amongst them: 100% authenticity. They knew their flaws and shortcomings but fully embraced who they were, what they stood for, and how they were going to show up in the world. This approach draws admiration, respect, and awe from the rest of us who haven't reached such elevated heights of success.

Strong team leaders can motivate and guide their business teams; they complete tasks and make decisions effectively. Whether the team chooses its leader, or you appoint one, no single leadership approach guarantees success. A team that does well with a strong leader may fail under the guidance of someone with a less effective leadership style. However, by understanding team leadership styles, you can work with your team leaders to help them overcome problems.

Although you probably have a natural leadership type, you may need to adopt characteristics from any of the types outlined based on the situation at hand or the people involved. For example, embracing an authoritarian style may be effective in an emergency, but when you've volunteered to lead a committee, choosing the servant leadership style will probably serve you better.

I appreciate there are plenty of other interpersonal traits that are equally important to be aware of such as assertiveness, emotional intelligence, creativity and attitude etc. but I have chosen to focus on the areas that I believe are pivotal to your inner compass. In the next chapter, I share the key areas in business that have a profound effect on how well you are able to navigate career success.

Compass Calibration: Explore the topics along with the tools and models here to determine which areas require greater attention.

Modus operandi: Ask yourself *"How well am I leveraging my interpersonal skills in life? Do I have blind spots, am I distorting them and what aspects do I need to improve on?"*

- Determine where your natural approach to risk is using Jumpstone's risk model
- Use the Mindset Continuum to assess where you are across various scenarios.
- Use the binary extremes exercise to determine if you have any extreme biases.
- Assess your ability to communicate effectively.
- Identify your leadership style and evaluate your ability to leverage your style?
- Become aware of any other interpersonal skills that are hindering progress.

CHAPTER 6

HOW TO NAVIGATE YOUR BUSINESS OPERANDI

"Hi, my name is Geoff and I run a family dry cleaning business offering excellent customer service."

"Shouldn't you anyway?" I silently comment to myself.

I can't tell you the number of times I've heard this type of pitch at a networking event. It is bland, ineffective, and doesn't compel anyone to use their business. I want to know what their real unique selling propositions are and what differentiates them from the competition! I want them to provoke a reaction; to inspire, engage, and compel us to learn more!

If you imagine a business like an archery target, it's the centre that you should be focusing on. *What is your core business? Why do you do what you do? Why are you different? What are your differentiators, and do you have a viable business model that offers a valuable product or service while making a decent margin!*

I've met too many business owners, start-ups, and entrepreneurs who are dabbling on the periphery. They spend far too much time focusing on superficial areas, such as business cards, creating an aesthetically pleasing website, networking events, social media campaigns, the list goes on... but all these activities are largely irrelevant if you haven't worked out the *core* of your business and how you are going to penetrate the market.

Find Your Arrowhead

I don't typically focus on the financial side of the business with my clients as there are plenty of more qualified and experienced coaches who can. However, an area that I am experienced and passionate about is brand. It's not unusual for me to find that a client hasn't really grasped the entirety of their brand and very often hasn't identified their unique selling points or expertise. Therefore, they are unable to leverage anywhere near the potential growth for their business.

For a visual explanation of this exercise, please go to the following URL on Jumpstone International's website to see the 2 minute coaching clip "Find your Arrowhead"

> URL: https://jumpstoneinternational.com/innercompass-resource/
> Website Resource Password:
> Inner-Compass72!

When I met Jonathan, he was no different than many business owners. He was offering a wide range of IT services from website design to SEO advice, thinking he would capture all sorts of clients and business opportunities. The reality was a sparse calendar of work that was a sporadic mix of contracts, providing him with thin margins.

It's like firing 100 arrows in the air hoping to find a target versus a trained hunter needing only one arrow to hit the bullseye.

I totally understand why business owners do this. I was one of the worst culprits at the outset of my business too, but I learnt fast that offering too many products and services simply confused my potential clients and diluted my offering and expertise.

I use a simple triangular model to explain how businesses are very often using the broad base of a triangle to capture the market (jack of all trades approach) instead of flipping it 180° to the narrow point, arrow heading with their expertise.

I shared with Jonathan another quick but highly effective model in identifying your ideal offering. Imagine a grid with various headings that allow you to determine the impact in your offering such as Profit, Expertise, Enjoyment, Uniqueness, Time, Resources, Skillset, Risk, Impact, etc. along the top of the grid.

Then, down the side, create several rows listing the various product offerings you provide to prospective clients. All you simply need to do is give yourself a gut score out of 10 as you go along each of the categories. What quickly emerges and becomes evident are the high and low scores that illustrate which of the products or services you should be focusing on, and which ones you should be letting go of. This method allows you to swiftly arrowhead your offering and align your brand with the products that highlight your expertise.

In Jonathan's case, he quickly saw his expertise was in SEO optimisation; he could create a far more profitable income stream versus labouring for hours over websites that he wasn't very good at.

Julie was another client who swiftly saw the benefit of this approach. She worked in real estate and was struggling to acquire prospective clients due to her shotgun approach. She had defaulted to the industry norm by creating business cards with her photo, highlighting the fact that she did commercial and residential for properties ranging from $100,000 to $5,000,000, from San Antonio to Austin. Her offering was so broad and bland that there wasn't any compelling reason why anyone would be attracted to her real estate services. As soon as she switched and focused on a particular niche in heritage homes in the historic district of downtown San Antonio, it was like bees to honey. Customers identify with expertise and are more inclined to pay for it too. It gives them the confidence that you are a genuine expert at what you do as you've proverbially hung your hat on your niche!

Understanding Brand

Glenn knew he had the knowledge, the skills, and the business acumen... So why wasn't his business taking off? He'd read countless business books and was following all the advice he'd sourced ready for his start-up venture–So, why was it stuck in first gear?

When I met Glenn, he shared with me that his annual turnover was $25,000. He was saddled with thousands of dollars of debt and barely scraping by, but he was determined to make a success of his security business. I have to say, I've developed a sixth sense for those who seem to 'have it' and Glenn certainly struck me as in that category so I was more curious than normal to discover what would materialise.

We took the usual E3 approach and swiftly moved to the challenges of his business and what immediately became obvious was his misguided obsession with the competition. He had been meticulous in his pricing and had positioned himself in the mid-range market despite being a start-up. His frustration was that he was spending countless hours pointing out the failings of his competition. I suggested that he might do better to pivot 180° and, instead, focus on his unique offerings and let the competition worry about themselves.

Unique selling propositions are part of my six-step branding model that illustrates how you differentiate yourself from the competition with confidence.

"Surely pointing out the competition's shortcomings illustrates why I'm better!" Glenn said to me.

Perhaps, but I pointed out that it also creates a negative vibe or persona around your business as you're focusing on the *negative* rather than the positive of what you have to offer. Prospective clients want to see what you have to offer versus badmouthing of the competition. When you spend time talking down your competition, people will begin to wonder what it is that you are hiding.

I suggested to Glenn that while it's all well and good to be aware of the competition, he should ignore them in terms of his marketing. Instead, focus on your unique selling propositions; what are you doing that stands out from the crowd, benefits the customers, and exceeds their expectations?

This imparts a level of trust and confidence in the customer's ability to make the right choice in terms of who they do business with. From that moment forward, Glenn set out with renewed focus to highlight his offering and all the security features and detail that highlight his services. It wasn't long before clients sat up and took notice, starting to invest in Glenn's security business. Glenn's natural business acumen allowed him to streamline his services and create a unique CRM platform, allowing for swift expansion across various towns, cities, and states within months. He explained it usually took years to get a foothold in a state before you can consider going out of state, but his model severely disrupted the market (like Netflix to Blockbuster) and swiftly grew.

His new approach brought in positive, upbeat customers who could see the true value in Glenn's offering despite the cost being higher than the competition. In less than three years, Glenn is running a vibrant, rapidly expanding business that is currently valued at over $3 million. I have no doubt he will become the future Securitas of the security world.

Sometimes, all it takes is a nudge to create the snowball effect and Glenn now sees with vivid clarity how his original approach was leaving him in first gear, despite having all the gears to hand.

Many of my clients know there is a sticking point, hurdle, or barrier they need to get over or break down but can't put a finger on it. They're too close to it or can't see through the fog above their heads.

There could be many factors at play, especially if you've been in business a while, but one of the essential areas to nail is your brand offering. However, in order to truly leverage your brand, you must thoroughly understand the entirety of your brand and streamline it accordingly.

Most people know that brand is essentially a persona used to gain an edge over your competitors - often in a crowded marketplace. However, brand is also a much-confused and misunderstood term; for some it merely represents the logo, while others appreciate there is a much broader, deeper meaning to it. However, nearly all struggle to decipher what is and isn't relevant when trying to apply it to their business and marketing efforts.

Brand entirety represents everything to do with the product or service– from its visual appeal, price, quality, and customer service to the emotional, historical, cultural, and human experience in interacting with it. It is a psychological reaction (expectations, feelings, and emotions) by the consumer to a promise about the kind of product or experience they are purchasing, and how they expect to feel when they use it.

Brand identity (logos, typography, colours, packaging, and messaging) is essentially the veneer or visual identity to the core substance of the brand entirety.

If the *brand identity* is designed to reflect the true entirety of the brand, it can act as a convincing and compelling face of the brand - *or persona* - that directly aligns with its substance. However, far too many companies rush out to get a name and a funky logo before they have properly examined the core substance and meaning behind their brands – ending up with a logo that is off kilter from their substance – creating confusion and distrust in potential consumers.

In a world where quality and service are often determined by fine margins, it is vital that companies invest time, money, and thought into creating an effective brand with a distinctive angle to represent their product(s) or service(s).

Therefore, compiled below are the *Six Steps to Sharpening Your Brand* that have proved to be very powerful and effective in aligning numerous business brands, allowing them to gain an essential edge in the marketplace.

Jumpstone's 6 Step Branding Model©:

1. Your Why

What is your *why*? Clients and customers of today want to know your core beliefs, why you are in business, if you're ethical, and who else benefits beyond your profits. Ultimately, they want to be able to decide if they *identify* with your brand. E.g. Assess your immediate reaction to Coca Cola, Gillette, Peloton, Protein World, Breitling, Porsche, etc...

2. Your Promise

What is your overarching promise to your customers or clients? Is your offering crystal clear? Does it relate to your products and services? Is it aligned with your market niche and target audience, or are you taking a scatter-gun approach to be a *jack of all trades* and master of none, thereby diluting your expertise?

3. Unique Selling Propositions

What are the 3-5 distinct or unique selling propositions that set you apart? This goes beyond generalizations such as "great customer service" or "high quality"; it should drill into the specifics of your product or service to support your promise such as Virtual Outsourced Accounting, Revolutionary App, or Tactical Soundboard.

4. What is Your Story or Evidence?

If customers are to buy from you, they need to believe and trust in you! You may have hooked them with your *why* and your *promise* but today's savvy consumer is a lot more discerning and wants to know whether they can TRUST in you and your product/service claims. Key trust points include experience, expertise, passion, and agreeing with your *why*.

5. Visual Identity

Is the visual identity in sync with the nature of your business? The logo should act as a veneer to the psychology or core substance of your brand. Therefore, it's key that every heading has a distinct thread running through it, aligning everything from your *why* to your *story*. Ask your clients and customers if they 'get it' or if they are left confused. They must be able to resonate with the design, colours, font, style, and messaging of your visual identity and how it relates to the core substance of your brand (i.e. headings 1 to 4).

6. Consistent Messaging

What is the *key message* to support your promise? You should aim to circle the brand with a supporting statement that links and reinforces your promise. Too many companies say too many things and dilute their message, but if you provide one consistent, succinct message (called a microscript) then you will strengthen your brand!

If someone says Nike, we all know its 'Just Do It!'

Now try Under Armour...Any Luck?

Not to do Under Armour any disservice but I suspect you didn't know. See my point!

(For those who want to know it's 'The only way is through')

"Branding is what you do, not what you call it."

—Jason Cohen

In summary, although brand identity is obviously easier to create and align from the start-up phase, many companies can still rectify glaring errors in their brands by examining these six headings to determine where to amend accordingly without the costly need to rebrand entirely.

The pivotal question for any business owner is this: is it the external circumstances of the environment that is affecting my business or role or me as the individual in question who is saying, doing, or operating in such a way that is creating friction and unintentional results?

It often helps to step back and evaluate the following

- **Are we leveraging our expertise? (Jack of all trades versus expert)**
- **Are we arrow-heading this expertise effectively in the marketplace?**
- **Are we aligning our strengths, leadership and personality to best effect?**
- **Are we delegating and outsourcing appropriately?**

Stephanie is a powerhouse. A true visionary with a buzzing flow of business, she has a good number of clients and a range of interesting projects. Whenever I met with her, she was working on a new initiative and raving about the opportunities it would bring. However, she also felt held back. She felt like she was pulling a heavy sledge. *Why? How?* I'd ask. "My team!" she replied.

She was totally frustrated she couldn't transfer the same natural motivation she had to members of her team. *Why was this area of the business so hard? Why did she find it so hard to connect with her employees? Why was there high turnover and what could she do about it?*

I ran an exercise called, *where are you now?* with Stephanie. It allows you to self-calibrate a quick assessment on a whole range of business and interpersonal areas such as being a leader, handling stress, and delegation by giving yourself a score out of 10. What became evident for Stephanie was her overwhelming confidence (erring on arrogance) for the majority of the business functions– except for relationship-based interpersonal skills.

I asked why she was managing the staff. "Well, I'm the CEO, that's what I should be doing!" "Really? Who says?" I asked.

"Well, if I'm the CEO, I'm meant to be the leader!"

I advised Stephanie to adopt a slight shift in her leadership approach. Why not be the visionary CEO and employ someone to be the manager of the business? Someone who you can relate to but has the responsibility and task to keep the team motivated – clearly a skillset that isn't in your natural wheelhouse.

"I can do that?" she asked.

"Sure, why not? It's your business, you're the CEO and you have the leeway to choose how best to operate your business. The only problem I see is you have become a slave to the word *should*," I explained.

So many people are constricted by the word *should*: by what they think they *should* be doing and what others expect of them. Rather than thinking, what's best for *me*, my staff, and the business? In Stephanie's case, she was not sidestepping or shirking her responsibilities, she was merely leveraging her true skill set in the best way possible for the business.

It may be that you're not good with figures, in which case, hire an accountant rather than struggle through on your own. Maybe you can't draw for toffee. If that's the case, use an online service such as Fiverr to create your own logo rather than taking weeks to learn an online tool like Canva.

One of the fastest and simplest ways to learn how to leverage your skillset is to take the online Strengths Test with Gallup which I outlined in chapter 3. Gallup introduced StrengthsFinder in the 2001 management book, *Now, Discover Your Strengths*. The book ignited a global conversation helping millions discover their top five talents. In "StrengthsFinder 2.0, Gallup unveiled the new and improved version of its popular online assessment.[1]

It primarily focuses on understanding your strengths so you can unlock your potential, leading you to greater performance.

Most people are taught to work on their weaknesses; to *fix* them. Instead, Gallup believes people should be learning how their strengths can overshadow their weaker areas. As Gallup says: "*Being well-rounded doesn't necessarily lead to*

[1] Gallup Strengths Finder: URL:

higher performance. You can achieve the highest levels of success only when you stop trying to be a little bit good at everything and instead hone what you are naturally best at."

I merely imparted the wisdom of Gallup onto Stephanie. As a result, she has freed up her time, stepped more into her visionary leadership, and allowed her team to flex their wings.

> **What could you be doing better by letting go, focusing on your strengths and allowing others to leverage theirs?**

But what if it isn't the individual and you recognise it's the company culture? While the brand model helps clients to determine how sharp their arrowhead is in terms of penetrating the market, the company culture model can help you pinpoint where the friction is coming from.

Company Culture Model

The **company culture model** was born out of helping one of my clients called Libby King clear the fog above her head. As I sketched out the position, circumstances, and dynamic of her company, I realised I'd created a template model that could be applied to other business out there.

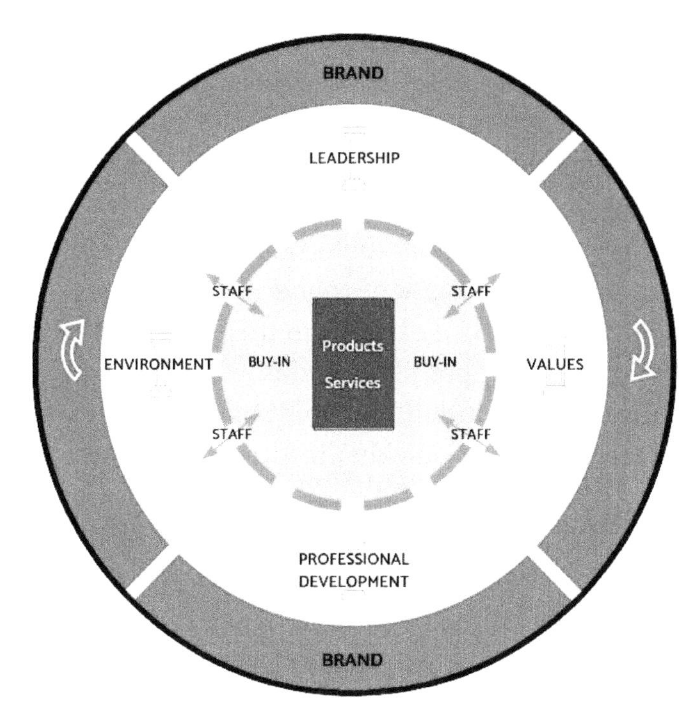

Company Culture Model
Dynamic relationship between Product, People and Brand

For a closer view and video explanation of this tool, please go to the following URL on Jumpstone International's website to see the 2 minute coaching clip **'Crack Your Company Culture'**

URL: https://jumpstoneinternational.com/innercompass-resource/
Website Resource Password:
Inner-Compass72!

In a nutshell this is how it works:

The company culture model illustrates the relationship between product, staff and brand allowing you to easily identify where things may be working and where they may be out of kilter.

The core represents the product or services that a company is leveraging. Around the outside are the employees who either buy-in to the ethos, why, and vision of the company or feel lost, disillusioned, or confused. It is a dotted line as it can flow either way. Company turnover quickly illustrates which way the flow of staff is going. If it is high, staff are obviously looking to exit. If it is low, this is either a promising indication of buy-in or may be explained by an exceptionally strong pillar such as strong leadership or a happy vibrant environment. There are **four key pillars** that influence the strength of the culture.

1. **Leadership Pillar.** *How effective and respected is the leadership and how well have they communicated their vision to the staff?*

2. **The Environment Pillar** represents what physical and mental environment they are providing for employees. To expand, the physical represents the location of the office whether it's a rural or urban location, how modern the building and its facilities are, how spacious or cramped it is and the overall infrastructure i.e.,

whether it's an open-plan or individual offices, whether there are chill out areas, refreshments areas, outdoor areas, etc. The mental environment is what type of atmosphere they intentionally provide for staff; what Google refers to as "psychological safety." Are staff members free to express themselves? To be listened to, heard, and respected? Or is there a toxic backstabbing environment where everyone is looking over their shoulders, wondering who said what about whom?

3. **The Values Pillar** refers to the values the company has agreed to live by as part of their culture. Companies often go to great lengths to agree and articulate the values but fail to live by them while others may not articulate them at all but because healthy values have been ingrained from the start and onboarded with new staff, there is a healthy culture at play.

   One size doesn't fit all here, but it is crucial that all staff are cognisant of living by agreed values where possible as this feeds into a happy, thriving environment where staff can be productive rather than being side-tracked by unhealthy practices that have crept into the workplace.

4. The final pillar is **personal development**. There are many companies out there that lose good staff members because they have failed to create avenues or pathways for staff to progress. I have heard far too many times that employees would love to stay but feel obliged to move on because they recognize they will stagnate or get left behind if they stay.

All the pillars are surrounded by how the company embraces their brand. If their brand is clear and concise to all, it helps staff buy into leveraging the product or service. If the brand is wishy washy or has evolved too many times that it has lost any coherent bearing on what the company is selling or offering as a service, staff again are lost as to how they fit into the picture. The 6 step branding model explained earlier can be used to assess how well the brand is understood internally for buy-in and externally for customers.

Teamwork

Team building and teamwork skills are critical for your effectiveness as a leader, manager, or entrepreneur. Even if you aren't yet in a leadership role, better understanding of teamwork can make you a more effective employee and give you an extra edge in your office. Team building success is when your team can accomplish something bigger and work more effectively than a group of the same individuals working on their own. You have a strong synergy of individual contributions. But there are two critical factors in building a high-performance team:

1. The first critical factor of teamwork success is that all the team efforts are directed towards the same clear goals: the team goals. This relies heavily on good communication within the team and harmony across the relationships.
2. The second important factor is the diversity of skills and personalities. When people use their strengths in full, it helps compensate for each other's weaknesses.

Here are some clear steps to building a strong, cohesive, and effective team:

1. Make sure **team goals are totally clear** and completely understood and accepted by each team member.
2. Make sure there is complete **clarity in who is responsible for what**. Do your best to avoid overlaps of authority. For example, if there is a risk that two team members will be competing for control in a certain area, try to divide that area into two distinct parts and give each more complete control in one of those parts,

according to those individual's strengths and personal inclinations.

3. For issues that rely on the team consensus and commitment, involve the whole team in the **decision-making** process. For example, use group sessions with collective discussions of possible decision options or solution ideas. What you want is for each team member to feel his or her ownership in the final decision, solution, or idea. The more he or she feels this way, the more likely he or she is to agree with and commit to the decided line of action.

4. Make sure there are **no blocked lines of communications** and that you and your people stay fully informed.

5. **Build trust** with your team members by spending one-on-one time in an atmosphere of openness and honesty. Be loyal to your employees if you expect the same.

6. Allow your office team members to build trust and **openness between each other** in team building activities and events. Give them opportunities for extra social time with each other in an atmosphere that encourages open communication. For example, provide a group lunch on Fridays.

7. **Deal with interpersonal issues**. Recognize them early and deal with them till you come to a full resolution.
8. Never miss opportunities to **empower your employees**. Say thank you and show appreciation of an individual team player's work.
9. **Give balanced feedback**; good and bad. Do not limit yourself to negative feedback. Be fair. Whenever there is an opportunity, give positive feedback as well!
10. **Remember, several minds are better than one!** It's not always admirable to do it alone. It's a strength to ask for collective input and support in each of your endeavours towards a common goal. Finally, although teamwork and team building can be challenging, the rewards from high team effectiveness are well worth it and will lead to greater personal and team success.

If you would like to learn more about teamwork, I highly recommend looking at Google's 2 year groundbreaking study *'Secrets of Successful Teamwork'* which examined the key elements to a successful thriving business.

Delegation Model

Delegation is the shifting of authority and responsibility for functions, tasks, or decisions from one person to another. As our careers evolve, this skill becomes more crucial. Otherwise, we are either too bogged down in the minutia of the business or way too above the action to have any influence due to a lack of perspective or overarching view to be strategic. The key is to work within the veneer between the two dimensions.

For a video explanation of this exercise, please go to the following URL on Jumpstone International's website to see the 2 minute coaching clip **'How to Delegate Effectively'**

URL: https://jumpstoneinternational.com/innercompass-resource/
Website Resource Password:
Inner-Compass72!

The delegation model explains how when we first start out, we have a narrow field of responsibility but a depth to our role. As we get promoted, it gets harder and harder to deliver to the same depth. We may succeed at first by working longer and longer hours and working to our max, but we can only sustain this level for a certain period before experiencing stress, overload, and burnout.

Effective managers learn to step up and empower the more junior members to take responsibility where they once were, while dipping in here and there to clarify or steer accordingly. Those managers that take a step too far above are accused of being distant, absent, or only present for their own gain. Those who remain in the detail are accused of being micro managers obsessed with their input, direction, and constant review of delegated work. The art of delegation is therefore in finding the balance between the two.

Those at the CEO level of multinational companies who are admired and respected, leaving others in awe of their ability to juggle so many competing demands, have often mastered this technique where they are operating with a very fine veneer between the two dimensions.

So, how do you hone this skill?

There is no one solution as there are far too many factors at play as to why managers and leaders may or may not be effective at delegating. It may be that they feel superior or more competent than their direct reports. Maybe they're more concerned at the thought of dumping work on others, have control tendencies, or simply lack assertiveness.

A common reason is the mistaken belief that a manager or leader has to be the expert over any subordinate before they can delegate. This is simply not true and a road to overload. In fact the higher up you go, the more you need to learn the art of delegating to another's strength or expertise. The Leadership Circle tool clearly illustrates the more a leader is able to step over the line of vulnerability and accept that they are not always best placed or the expert to do a certain job, project or task – the more they will excel in their leadership.

Whatever it is, the Pathfinder Model allows individuals to assess which factors are at play such as their conditioning, modus operandi, strengths and skill set, approach to risk, binary extremes, aspirations, leadership style and drive to unravel the root causes. Again, awareness leads to understanding which in turn leads to action in adjusting their ability to balance operating in the veneer to delegate more effectively.

Intercultural Understanding

There is a vast library of knowledge and theory out there on this subject, but there is a particular exercise that can immediately open your eyes to the vast differences in the lens we wear based on our cultural upbringing. Unless you have travelled much or worked in intercultural environments, it is very likely that you have more of a monocultural mindset and are ignorant or blind to some of the more obvious factors at play. Our world is so connected physically, geopolitically, and digitally that it is vital we aim to gain a greater awareness of overarching differences at play.

For a video explanation of this exercise, please go to the following URL on Jumpstone International's website to see the 2 minute coaching clip **'Understanding your Cultural Orientation'**

> URL: https://jumpstoneinternational.com/innercompass-resource/
> Website Resource Password:
> Inner-Compass72!

The tool works by simply placing a vertical line between the opposing ends of a particular dimension such as individualism versus collectivism or formal versus informal. After evaluating several dimensions, you will end up with a graph that illustrates where you lie across each dimension. What is plain to see is anywhere where you might have a very strong leaning to one end of a dimension. This isn't particularly a bad thing, but it might help explain why you struggle to connect with another individual who is at the opposite end to you. Now imagine if you have 3 or 4 of these dimensions in contrast to another individual. This explains the friction and conflict we often encounter due to intercultural differences rather than a personality clash. It works rather like the earlier binary extremes exercise but for cultural differences and is excellent at breeding fresh perspective and compassion in working with international counterparts.

Now that we've looked at aspects of your individual contribution to the business as well as the broader business dynamic of culture, brand and teamwork, how do you determine if it's the business that needs an overhaul or your own modus operandi? This is extremely tough to determine on your own. You're simply too close to it. You need to step back to gain perspective. You can do this to some extent through the tools and exercises I've shared but an easier and more accurate evaluation would be to use a coach to professionally soundboard your specific challenges.

At this point, I would also like to share a personal lens on the crucial aspects I consider to be vital in doing business.

Back in 2015, I was a keynote speaker in Kazakhstan for an international global forum for their elite leaders in industry. I was asked to provide perspective and insight into how their senior leaders could effectively raise their game to the chief executive level. Nature is my go to for inspiration, so I took to the Austrian mountains and reflected on all the theory and experience I've gained across various industries and management roles. What emerged were several key elements that I turned into an acronym called: "**What STIICX in Business.**"

It stands for **Signature, Teamwork, Intent, Instinct, Confidence and Flexibility.**

Leadership Signature

Leadership signature is your personal brand or style that suits you.

Theory:

- Great leaders create a vision of the future that is vivid and compelling, motivating employees to want to achieve it, but it's their leadership brand that conveys their identity and distinctiveness as a leader. It communicates the value they have to offer.
- If you have the wrong leadership brand for the position you have, or the position you want, then your work is not having the impact it could.
- A strong personal leadership brand allows you to be distinctive and stand out and become known to your colleagues.
- Creating a leadership brand gives you *focus.* When you clearly identify what you want to be known for, it is easier to let go of the tasks and projects that do not let you deliver on that brand. Instead, you can concentrate on the activities that *do.*

My point is most of us want to work for a company that makes a difference in the world as well as having an impact on its customers and communities. So...

- Discover or identify your personal brand - your signature!
- Don't try and copy someone else.
- Be prepared to stand out and be different and be confident when you're right.
- Be proud of what you have to offer and find what makes you comfortable in your own skin. ***Consider this: If you're not comfortable, why would others follow you?***

Teamwork

Theory: Business is built on a solid foundation of relationships and trust. Without these two things, you can't have a business– or at least not a successful business. Take time every day to build relationships with the members of your team, your customers and vendors, your boss and your boss's boss, others in your industry, and your community. The stronger your relationships, the better a leader you will be.

Case study: I think there is no better analogy of teamwork than an F1 pit stop. These guys race an average of 60 laps, covering 200 miles in almost two hours– and yet the difference between first and second often comes down to just a couple of seconds in the pits. Anything longer than 10 seconds and you've almost certainly lost the race. However, while being a great example of teamwork, it still feels too distant from the average working life.

Let's look at another example: The St. Gilgen Fire Brigade. I used to live in a small village called St. Gilgen, which lies at one end of a lake in the Austrian Alps. There are no paid firefighters and yet, every single person who lives there is safe in the knowledge that if any fire breaks out, the villagers will pull together and react with lightning speed to assist. Every single one of them knows that their role – however large or small – contributes to the bigger picture and ultimately means the safety and lives of the village. Now that's teamwork! The key is that every single person knows next time it could be their house or business up in flames.

Point: Look at any acceptance speech of a famous sportsman or actor and you'll nearly always see that they thank their team. They recognise that without the effort and hard work of their team, they would never be in that position in the first place. So, if you can create teamwork in your staff where everyone wants to support each other because they know it contributes to their success too, you'll have achieved a team mentality in everything they do, and it will provide a much greater chance of success for all.

Intent

Theory: Felix Baumgartner's intent was to break the world record for the highest and fastest freefall above earth. Every single member of his team knew what his aim was, which fed into every single detail in the preparations, but here's the key: He didn't instruct them on their expertise. His expertise was to jump, but the team's expertise was to put him in position to do so!

Instead of giving instructions, give INTENT. Your team members will stop requesting permission and start thinking for themselves to discover the answers. You'll change from being the 'answer man' to giving them psychological ownership and responsibility of their own actions while providing a leadership steer to their INTENT. This inspires them to do the best job they can and take ownership rather than offset the responsibility or blame onto someone else. In return, they gain the respect and acknowledgement of their skill.

JFK's 'we choose to go to the moon' is an incredible example of a speech that inspired intent– and it was over 50 years ago!

The two key pillars that need to be in place for INTENT to work are 'Technical Competence' and

'Organisational Clarity.' Whenever one of your team members asks you a question, simply respond by asking, '*Is it the right thing to do?*' You'll both know and will keep you on course to deliver!

Point: Give control to others to build leaders.

Of course, this is difficult as it goes against the grain of what we've been taught growing up. We've been led to believe we should *take control* and attract followers... but it's far more effective to give control and create leaders.

Whether it's 2 or 2,000 minds– more minds are better than one! Any organisation or industry with this mindset has beaten the competition because ***they're working as a team with real intent!***

Instinct is often overlooked or forgotten but it is a vital aspect of business management.

Instinct

- When leading a team through uncharted waters, there is no roadmap on what to do. Everything is uncertain, and the higher the risk, the higher the pressure. That is where your natural intuition must kick in.
- Guiding your team through the process of your day-to-day tasks can be honed down to a science. But when something unexpected occurs,

or you are thrown into a new scenario, your team will look to you for guidance.

- Drawing on experience is a good reflex but when faced with tough decisions, you will need to depend on your gut instinct for answers.
- Learning to trust yourself is as important as your team learning to trust you.

After completing our six-week project to protect the watershed of the local villages, 25 trekkers and my leadership team set off on a two-week expedition to discover Hells Gate Falls on the Mullins River in the Belizean jungle.

No one had ever set eyes on these waterfalls, and it was our clear intention to cross uncharted terrain and be the first to do it. All went well until the final day. We didn't realise the waterfalls sat in a valley over 300 metres deep with sheer jungle-vined walls. I went ahead to check out the situation and made it to the valley floor and I was elated at the roaring sound of the waterfalls just metres around the rockface. The only way to view it was to swim across the fast-flowing river.

Here comes the dilemma: Do I take the risk, win bravado points, and claim a first, or turn back knowing I'm unlikely ever to get another chance?

I'd navigated uncharted terrain for nine days to reach this point. We'd suffered a forest fire en-route, a few minor injuries, and a couple of detours but I was now almost within touching distance – just 20m to my goal. I could hear the thunderous volume of water cascading into the unknown. However, the river was simply too dangerous to cross and, despite an almighty urge to have a crack at it, instinct kicked in, telling me that I would be swept over to my death, leaving the team exposed and without a leader at the top.

That was the closest we came to seeing the falls, but I have no regrets. In fact, I'm proud I made the right call and that we made it as far as we did and I've lived to tell the tale.

Point: The key' is to learn to trust your *gut instinct*. Even though external pressures may be egging you on to complete that project or fire that employee– whatever circumstance may be, take a step back and learn to trust your instincts by evaluating the best course of action. It may not be life-threatening, but it may just save your career.

Confidence

Develop the confidence and character to stand up for what you think because that's better than always being a 'yes' man and staying safe with the crowd.

Business case: Let's say you've been tasked with delivering a project within a week, but you know that your team will need two weeks. Don't offset the problem to a subordinate so that it becomes their problem– stand up and manage up. Give sound reasoning as to why you need two but then ensure you deliver.

Confidence is necessary to convey your identity and distinctiveness as a leader as it communicates the value you offer. Confidence, together with your leadership brand, allows all that's powerful and effective about your leadership to become known to your colleagues, enabling you to generate maximum value.

Various leaders and visionaries have become famous because they have totally and utterly conveyed 100% confidence in their beliefs and goals in life.

- As a leader, you will have days where things aren't going according to plan. This is true with any business, large or small, but your job as a leader is to put out fires and maintain team morale.
- Your job as a leader is to keep up your confidence level and assure everyone that setbacks are natural; the important thing is the broader goal.
- As a leader, aim to deliver consistency in your leadership style. If the team knows and

understands your leadership brand, they know where they stand and, in turn, will gain greater confidence themselves.

Steve Jobs was an American entrepreneur, marketer, and inventor, and the cofounder, chairman, and CEO of Apple Inc. Through Apple, he was widely recognized as a charismatic and design-driven pioneer of the personal computer revolution and for his influential career in the computer and consumer electronics fields, transforming "one industry after another," from computers and smartphones to music and movies.

He has been referred to as a "**legend,**" a "**futurist,**" and a "**visionary**." He has been described as a "Father of the Digital Revolution," a "master of innovation," "the master Evangelist of the digital age," and a "design perfectionist."

Steve Jobs once said, *"Customers don't know what's best for them."*

They didn't know they needed Apple products until they were introduced into the world! Now it sounds like arrogance, but it's confidence when you can deliver.

While Jobs was clearly talented, I doubt he would have gotten anywhere near as far without his signature leadership style, self-belief, intent, and confidence.

Flexibility

- It's no secret that the business environment for most companies is changing faster than ever before, requiring people and the organisations they work for to change right along with it.
- We've all been faced with situations where it feels like bullets are flying at us but great leaders see the changes coming on the horizon. They constantly push their team and organisations to be in the right place when those changes happen.
- You need to be able to 'think on your feet' and flex to the situation at hand, knowing when to deviate from the original plan.

'What STIICX in business' has helped many individuals and businesses calibrate their overall operational effectiveness alongside using the various tools in leadership, culture and brand to address specific areas that need attention.

Hopefully by now you are gaining a valuable lens on the insights needed to navigate a path to your true north. However, you probably have a few hurdles you might need to overcome in being able to move forwards which we will examine in the next chapter.

Compass Calibration: There are so many components to business success, it seems superficial to narrow it down to a few key components. However, these areas highlighted above so often explain the barriers to success that it is vital that they are understood in order to move forward. In summary:

- What is your arrowhead?
- How effective is your company culture?
- Do you truly understand your brand?
- Are you employing the principles of teamwork?
- Do you know how to lead with intent and delegate accordingly to leverage expertise?
- Are you aware of intercultural differences to operate effectively in today's globalised marketplace?

CHAPTER 7

HOW TO OVERCOME YOUR HURDLES

Marissa was hugely talented but *frustrated.* She'd worked in the White House as a research intern for the Obama administration and gained huge insight and experience into the wheels of government.

When I met her, Marissa was on a part-time sojourn with the San Antonio city council, trying to gain inroads into a more established career. "I don't get it," she said. "I have all this experience and energy to offer and I can't seem to get noticed."

"Well, what have you tried so far?" I asked.

I soon discovered she had been taking the *reactive* approach. Waiting for feedback, waiting to be asked to be involved in projects, waiting to be included in pivotal meetings, etc.

"Why don't you take a more proactive approach?" I suggested. "Why not draw up a job spec that outlines exactly what you're capable of and how you can dovetail in the missions and objectives of the city council?"

"Am I *allowed* to do that?" she asked.

"No one says you can't, and you don't know unless you try! You might even be saving your boss a headache. They often have so much on their plates that they don't have sufficient time to be on the lookout for *your* career; they're too busy navigating theirs. But if you play a card that can *solve* one of their challenges, the response is likely to be positive."

Two weeks later, Marissa came bounding into the conference room and said, "Guess what? I've been offered the position!"

"Of course, you have," I said. "You merely shone a light on what they couldn't see! Brilliant, well done, I'm so proud of you and excited for your prospects!"

You see, too many people conform to an HR process that's been created to help filter out viable candidates which often works. However, it doesn't allow for the best candidates who often have the extra edge because they've done something a little different to give them an edge but doesn't necessarily fit the

HR mold. In fact, who does? Therefore, companies often end up with the safe bet rather than the *best* bet. But it's either too hard to find the golden nugget or too risky. Those of us who understand one must put themselves forward and get creative are those who often appear to "get lucky" but have actually cracked the code of how to bypass HR systems to land the job of their dreams.

Training and Qualifications

It may be that you need to get more qualified, gain a certificate or an accreditation to prove your skills. The key is in determining if you really need to invest the time and effort into gaining an extra qualification or if you are simply falling into the trap of imposter syndrome, failing to recognise you already have the skills and depth of experience.

I have met with countless clients who consider earning an MBA without really knowing *why* or what they will gain from the huge investment and countless hours of study to largely replicate what they've done for years. If it is of genuine interest, then great, go ahead and you'll likely enjoy and benefit from doing the coursework. However, if it is merely done to fill the void of doubt, it will likely be a painful experience both financially and mentally with no real results other than another certificate to pepper the wall.

Politics

Perhaps you find it difficult to navigate office politics. This is an inescapable part of working in an organisation that either hinders or leverages your career. *Why is it that some people seem to expertly navigate the complex array of personalities, hierarchies, and departments while others are left scratching their heads, wondering why they are side-lined or not recognized for the value they bring to the organisation?* This points back to the key question of determining whether it is the company culture and the circumstances of your role, or your own personality. *Are you aiding your career path or are you sabotaging your career ladder opportunities by clashing with pivotal and influential managers?*

Influence

Too many people believe influence is a skill you either have or you don't, much like trait theory in leadership. The fact is, there is a science to being persuaded and the more you learn about this topic, the more you're likely to leverage opportunities that you deserve with an ethical helping hand from science.

When deciding, it would be nice to think that people consider all available information in order to guide their thinking, but the reality is often very different. In our busy lives of information overload, we often look to short cuts to make decisions, and these heavily influence how we react.

Trust plays a big role in how effective you can be in a role; without it, there is very little chance that changes you need to make will be taken on board by others. Robert Cialdini's book, *Persuasion*, is one of the authoritative texts on the aspects of human interaction that involve six shortcuts as universals that guide human behaviour in influencing others. They are:

Reciprocity: Returning a gift, favour, or opportunity in kind.

Scarcity: People naturally want more of what is scarce.

Authority: People follow the lead of credible, knowledgeable experts.

Consistency: One action or commitment naturally leads to another.

Liking: Tune in to similarities, paying compliments and cooperation.

Consensus: Highlight what others are already doing.

If you would like to learn and understand more on this topic, Daniel Pink's work also explains how three fundamental human qualities – attunement (the ability to take another's point of view), buoyancy (remaining resilient in the face of rejection), and clarity (helping others make it through the "murk of information") — also lie at the heart of persuading, influencing, and moving people.

Circumstances

This is a very ambiguous heading, but your circumstances need to be evaluated in context as they are very likely unique in comparison to someone else's situation. If you are a single parent, or parents with disabled children relying on the local services or grandparents, then your options to relocate for a new job are very limited versus someone with no strings attached.

If you need to get qualified but can't afford the time or financial commitment this may hinder your progress versus someone who has just received a healthy redundancy with the time to study.

There are numerous other factors that could be at play such as time, family, culture, health, boss, qualification, experience, or even unplanned ones such as a pandemic. The key is not to ignore or be easily defeated by your circumstances, but to take a step back and fully evaluate your position. You can then use your creativity and resourcefulness along with other techniques, such as sound boarding with a trusted friend, Covey's 'Sphere of Influence' or talk to an expert or coach to examine and evaluate how you can best navigate around the hurdle or leverage a resource to enable you to do so. This naturally leads us to *mindset.*

Mindset

I know we touched on this in Chapter 5 but mindset is worth a deeper look as our mental approach is often the pivotal difference between success and failure.

> **"Whether you think you can, or you think you can't – you're right!"**
> ***— Henry Ford***

Mindset is a curious phenomenon, but many people aren't even aware of it or think to question it. They are operating in *default* mode. Therefore, they are unaware there may be some self-sabotage or false beliefs working behind the scenes to undermine their confidence. In Neuro Linguistic Programming (NLP) this is called meta-programs.

Meta-programs are powerful mental processes that influence and direct our decisions, behaviours, actions, and interactions with others. They determine how we interpret the world otherwise known as reality. They are like coding directing our beliefs, memories and thoughts and creating responses which we generalise, distort or even delete. They also operate at a subconscious level as the conscious mind can only pay attention to a limited amount of data at any one time - otherwise it would be exhausting.

However, this means meta programs become a default in how you think or act resulting in significant differences in behaviour from person-to-person. Meta-programs, also fluctuate depending on whether life is going well or if you are experiencing stress or emotional difficulties. The constant bombardment or sensory data is interpreted in a split second and your coding determines what you pay attention to or not.

Tony Robbins helps make this tangible by talking about matchers and mis-matchers. Matchers see the similarities in things while mis-matchers tend to see the differences. Neither is right or wrong but understanding an individual's approach to the world helps how you may react.

Matchers are often optimistic and tend to find similarities and common ground, so you'll be more successful reflecting their experiences, beliefs and perceptions. Mis-matchers are often more individualistic and tend to go against the grain. They tend to point out the differences or what they see wrong often creating tension in a team. However, they are extremely valuable in creating innovation and seeing fresh avenues so supporting and balancing both perspectives can create trust and balance while driving greater output and results overall.

Therefore, evaluating your own meta programs allows you to determine how useful they are and how they are shaping your life and circumstances. If you discover they are potentially sabotaging you, you might need to delve deeper into your root conditioning to unravel or unlock your meta programming.

As you become more aware you can re-code where relevant so you can elicit a more positive response. It will also help you become tuned in to other people and their psychological tendencies so you can calibrate your behaviour and better communicate your response in interacting with them.

It's not easy but as you learn to look for clues within a person's choice of words, their disposition and behaviour you will begin to see a marked improvement in your ability to react and improve relationships. The knock-on effect to your outlook and wellbeing is that you will naturally motivate and influence those around you too. There are various tools out there to help you achieve this.

James Anderson has created a brilliant model that uses the principles of mindset as set out by the pioneer Carol Dweck. It helps illustrate that mindset rather than being black and white, and is more akin to a continuum. We can therefore better assess where we lie on this continuum and how it fluctuates on a day-to-day basis. This allows us to see the meta patterns we may be falling into and whether we wish to make changes to better embrace areas of our lives.

This list of hurdles is by no means definitive and can include other factors such as our ability to influence, communicate, or lead. It often helps to refer to our modus operandi and what we learnt here to determine if there are any major hurdles we have to learn to overcome.

The final hurdle worth examining are our *circumstances*. Many of my clients often feel trapped by apparent circumstances and determine there is simply little or no way out of their situation. This very much plays into Covey's *Sphere of Influence*. He distinguishes between proactive people – who focus on what they can do and can influence – and reactive people who focus their energy on things beyond their control. Reactive people maintain an attitude of victimisation and blame. I don't wish to diminish or patronize my client's circumstances in any way, but there is very often a way out of the situation if you entertain the idea of a *solution*. It all starts with the right mindset and believing you can work towards a solution.

In my own life, I have been told countless times that it is not possible to achieve something because I don't have the skills, I don't have the connections, or I've left it too late. I've often felt the exception rather than the norm in challenging these beliefs but I'm fortunate in having a stubborn streak that refuses to admit defeat until at least I've given it a go. This key trait is often evident in entrepreneurs, visionaries and pioneers who are prepared to challenge the status quo or be prepared to disrupt the common consensus.

As if to illustrate my point, there are countless quotes that often make me smile and remind me that those in power are often the ones too blinded to see opportunity.

When Robert Fulton proposed the idea of a steamboat in the 1800s, it is said Napoleon Bonaparte retorted,

"How sir, would you make a ship sail against the wind and currents by lighting a bonfire under her deck? I pray you, excuse me, I have not the time to listen to such nonsense!

The president of the Michigan Savings Bank infamously told Horace Rackham (Henry Ford's lawyer),

"The horse is here to stay, but the automobile is only a novelty – a fad."

Incredibly in 1899, a commissioner of the U.S. Office of Patents, Charles H. Duell, said,

"Everything that can be invented has already been invented!"

It's astonishing as well as disheartening to read how many areas of our lives we are constrained and influenced by overconfident disillusioned individuals projecting their own blinded mindset.

It could of course also mean we have to find a way of expanding our minds or learning to adapt or flex towards a different approach. I have developed a unique method that helps illustrate the challenge and appreciate it is a work in progress versus the black or white approach of either - or!

Finding the Line

This exercise is very effective in learning how to take a new approach. The left side represents your current position while the right side illustrates where you are trying to get to. In the middle is what I call 'No Man's Land.' The next step is to list down the left-hand side various scenarios where you might encounter your challenge. The idea is that you must step into No Man's Land to learn how to navigate a new way of operating. The first time you try, you may strike out too far and retreat to the safety of your trench and stay there. i.e., once bitten twice shy.

However, just like the metaphor of getting back on a bike or a horse, it is crucial we step out and have another go. Eventually you will find a new line from where you can more confidently operate. The resulting graph looks like a DNA chart. This exercise has helped people pleasers become more assertive, imposter syndrome sufferers share their perspective and even egotistical leaders become humbler.

The key thing to remember is it is a work in progress – just like prototyping. You aren't going to get it right the first time. The other crucial factor is to remember self-compassion. The sheer fact that you are stepping out into No Man's Land should be recognised as bravery whatever the result. In time, you will make progress.

There may well be external hurdles at play too such as intercultural collectivism, society expectations and parental pressure. The truth is there could be an infinite list of hurdles that could be genuine or being used as an excuse, but they are all impacting on your ability to move forward. The crucial factor here is to pinpoint what it is and ask yourself the intelligent questions to determine how best to navigate under, over, around or through the challenge.

This leads us onto the next area of the Pathfinder Model and how we can best leverage **resources** available to us to help us realise our aspirations.

Compass Calibration: The key point here is to evaluate genuine versus perceived barriers and what is the swiftest and smartest way to navigate through them. Examine your mindset by asking the following:

- What fears, doubts, and insecurities are you hiding from?
- What are your genuine versus perceived barriers?
- Have you taken a step back to understand the scale of the hurdle?
- Are you being swayed by too many external 'shoulds' versus your intrinsic needs?

CHAPTER 8

HOW TO HARNESS YOUR RESOURCES

Back in 1998, I had a revolutionary idea that I felt would truly benefit the sewing community. I had observed how my girlfriend spent hours pinning and tracing out patterns, then laboriously marking a seam line before the various sections of a garment could be cut out. I naturally questioned whether there was a way to half the time in this process.

After employing the principles of design thinking, I developed a concept and thought I was ready to go to market with my idea. However, my naivety left me lost in the dark as my idea was rejected on the grounds that there wasn't a working prototype or a patent to protect it. Being short on funds and little knowledge in epoxy modelling, I felt I'd hit a brick wall. However, a chance meeting with a fellow Englishman called Geoff at my Swedish classes provided just the avenue to develop prototypes to illustrate the workings of the design. Geoff also knew about patents and helped me understand the principles of writing a patent. I set to, writing my own patent to support my invention. After a long two years, I finally had both a working protype and a patent in principle for The Saxtrack.

During this time, I had secured a job at Dyson, so I was able to bounce my patent off the company's patent attorney and check the validity of my application. The patent attorney gave it the thumbs up with a few minor tweaks and it was successfully sold to Husqvarna. On my 5 year journey I gained information from professionals, leant on fellow enthusiasts, sought advice from experts and tackled each obstacle with a can-do mindset.

This story illustrates the many hurdles faced in the journey to success and how without the aid and support of so many people involved, it would never have come to fruition. However, I was instrumental in leaning in on the resources available to me to make my vision a success.

So many individuals when faced with hurdles often stop or turn around and give up, but just as the proverb says: where there is a will there's a way. So often the key to success is keeping an open mind and examining where help could be at hand. If you adopt a proactive approach and a good dose of self-belief, imagine what you could achieve. Consider the following:

- **Where are you allowing yourself to believe there is no way forward?**
- **Are you being too reactive and waiting for others to aid or assist you?**
- **Who could aid you in gaining the knowledge or acquiring the right skill set?**

Again, it is important to reiterate that the Pathfinder Model Resources column is not a definitive list, but mere examples of what factors could be available to us in leveraging our path forwards. Some of my clients have objected at this point and said, "Isn't this using people?" This is an important note to observe as there are unscrupulous sorts out there who will indeed focus on who, what and where they can cheat the system for their own gains.

However, what I am talking about here is leveraging opportunity where it is available without compromising on your values or your scruples to gain ground. There are parallels to the binary extremes exercise here in that a fear of using or gaining advantage by unfair means, leads clients to deduce that they can't use any techniques, contacts, or avenues to give themselves a hand up. However, there is a line between the two extremes where you can be safe in the knowledge that it aligns with your moral compass.

As observed, too many people are reactive in their actions, hoping that others will give them the hand up needed. The truth is, very often you need to meet them halfway. It reminds me of a Ghanain I met who put his whole faith in God to help him find a job but who had made no job applications, ads, or any other effort to gain employment. I told him the joke about the chap who prayed to God to win the lottery and finally God came one day and said "At least meet me halfway and buy a lottery ticket!"

The point being is that too many individuals wait for things to happen rather than adopt the proactive mindset to think what can they do to aid their progression.

There are so many ways that you can help advance your career aspirations. Some of the suggestions on the Pathfinder Model resources column include:

Certificates: What qualifications or training might aid your career aspirations

Strategic Advances: Who can you reach out to that might aid your understanding or help advance your interests?

Mindset: Are you serving or sabotaging your aspirations. What mindset will best serve your goals and objectives in life?

New Projects (showcasing fresh skills): What projects, tasks or initiatives could you volunteer for or create that can showcase your hidden skills and potential?

Company Budget Where can you leverage funds to aid personal development? (ask if there isn't any!) Is there a personal development fund? Can HR aid you in getting qualified, taking a course or funding an initiative?

Cheerleaders (my personal favourite): Everybody has cheerleaders – those people who have seen the true genius within you and only want you to succeed. How can you lean and learn from them to help navigate potential opportunities?

Mentoring / Job shadowing: Who could you learn from? Where can you best channel your enthusiasm to aid others?

Succession Planning: What gaps do you need to fill in on your Present Day GPS? What areas might you need greater focus or improvement to become eligible for consideration?

Career Sabbatical: Would a break harness or hinder your career? Would a sabbatical in another area or department add to your strings?

Showcase Your Talent: What could you do to demonstrate your hidden talents? Maybe you could write a blog, create a podcast, interview people, take a survey, take psychometric tests, travel, take up a new sport or hobby that would showcase your determination, talent or aspiration? You don't know until you try.

The fact is, there is an endless list of initiatives you could undertake or implement but the myriad of choices often paralyses people into inaction until they find the perfect opportunity. In truth, it rarely emerges and so people trudge on with the status quo. It is those of you who have a go, try something new, dare to try that often accomplish things as it provides a catalyst to the next attempt until one day it threads all the other attempts together. There is rarely, if ever, overnight success, but the media portray a lie leaving people despondent when their first attempts don't turn out as they expected. The truth is all the attempts add up to the bigger picture until finally it all clicks into place when the time is right.

I often wonder if the digital social media that younger generations have only ever known, mean they are losing the ability to be tenacious and persistent in their endeavours. It reminds me of the story I read about Thomas Edison's trials and tribulations to invent the working light bulb.

In the period from 1878 to 1880, Edison and his associates worked on at least 3,000 different theories to develop an efficient incandescent lamp. Upon being asked how he felt about failing so many times he said,

> **"I have not failed 3,000 times—I've successfully found 3,000 ways that will not work."**

Compass Calibration: Are you trapped in a bubble focusing on the problem rather than asking intelligent questions to determine your solution?

- Have you explored all possible avenues to aid you in gaining momentum?
- Have you prioritized time and opportunities to gain ground in your goals?

CHAPTER 9

ALIGNING YOUR TRUE NORTH

I often share with my clients that all the elements at play are like looking at the stars, it's finding the constellations within them that is the key to understanding how they all interconnect. By this point of the book, you should have a very clear picture of your own constellations and what blind spots or areas of personal development might be needed.

I fully recognise that it can feel very overwhelming to comprehend all in one go. This is where the Pathfinder Model is instrumental in providing a map to understand your Present Day GPS and act as a guide to highlight areas which are in flow and areas that may be in friction. The main aim is to obviously to recalibrate your bearing so you can swing the needle towards your true north and in doing so gain the alignment and balance in life that so many yearn for.

As highlighted earlier in the book, the root challenge is to determine if it is external factors that are influencing current circumstances or your own modus operandi that is at hand.

Very often, there are elements that lie in both of these areas, so untangling the difference is the key to successfully moving forwards. The Pathfinder Model and the exercises contained within this book allow you to do just that.

Once you have gained clarity and direction, you will become empowered to take proactive action to cut a clear path towards reaching your full potential. For some it requires calculated tweaks here and there – much like a train grinding on the rails only needs a slight adjustment to run true. Others require more radical or drastic action to redress the balance which may require a change of roles, a change in company or even a new career path.

It is my fervent hope that this book helps you turn the lens so that you can gain a crystal-clear image of where you are and where you are aiming to go. The recalibration of your bearing to true north will allow you to move forward in the direction of your calling and align with your inner compass to live a more meaningful, productive, and happier life.

Compass Calibration: The more effort you put into aligning with your inner compass, the more likely you are to be happy in your vocation, flourishing in your wheel of life, leveraging your true potential, and living in balance with purpose.

I look forward to you resetting your bearing and achieving what I know is possible and has helped so many before you.

CHAPTER 10

CONCLUSION

> **"Do not go where the path may lead, go instead where there is no path and leave a trail."**
>
> ***—Ralph Waldo Emerson***

This quote is as apt today as it's always been. We are often conditioned and constrained to take the path of others, but we often celebrate those that dare to blaze a new trail. I took that risk and today, I am running a successful and impactful executive coaching business called Jumpstone International which is aligned with my five pillars.

My intrinsic motivations and inner calling align and dovetail with my personal and business aspirations. I am leveraging my true strengths and skill set and providing maximum impact for my clients while being rewarded for it. I am living in a rural location that provides both a healthy physical environment to flourish as well as a home that provides mental wellbeing where I can live by the values that I truly believe in and offer maximum focus to my clients.

It wasn't easy and it took me over 20 years to get here, but it is my fervent belief that you too can find your inner compass if you engage in the principles of this book so you can navigate to live aligned to your true north!

"Don't be pushed by your problems,
Be led by your dreams!"

Author unknown.

AUTHOR

Matt Guiver's unique approach to executive coaching, workshops and innovation provides swift clarity and insights for leaders and executive teams to take tangible action - providing transformative impact for months and years to come.

Matt's intrepid and natural curiosity for life has seen his 25 year career take on various leadership roles across numerous industries and sectors as well as work with a variety of multinationals such as Husqvarna, Dyson, SAP and Sitecore.

Matt graduated in Industrial design, helping him to form the backbone to his creative instincts. He has always been curious about what makes people tick and has become interculturally astute having driven many projects, partnerships and developments in over 35 countries spanning Asia, Africa, Europe and the Americas. Matt combines his first hand experience and creative flair with his qualifications and accreditations to help clients navigate their goals with a tactical soundboard . The clarity gained allows them to reach their goals in line with their true north.

For more inspiration to learn more about Matt Guiver and Jumpstone International's Executive Coaching Services, please go to www.jumpstoneinternational.com

I would like to express my appreciation and highly recommend working with Matt. His coaching is a precious gift; each session was like a refueling pitstop. It helped me pause and connect deeply with what works for me and what makes me tick. His coaching style adds a meaningful direction, it was a great journey!

Cansu Ciga Turkkan
– Head of Partner Recruitment,
EMEA South - SAP

I was working with Matt on on our European Managing Directors meetings. He was hired to provide us with a keynote speech about change-management followed by a guided workshop to evaluate the agility of the attendees to reach outstanding results. Matt was a tremendous help in the preparation of the meeting and very supportive with ideas and recommendations. The keynote and workshop was very well prepared and Matt was very focused on topic and timing. The group enjoyed his professionalism and I personally enjoyed the open communication, way beyond the original topic.

Rene Eisbrich
– Chief Operations Officer
at Lagermax Autologisti

I thoroughly recommend Matt. He takes time, shows a genuine interest in helping you as the coach explore what's important to you. Thought provoking and professional. Super flexible and able to pivot when the moment needs it to keep it fresh.

John Massey
– EMEA Head of Leaderership Development - SAP

Matt and I spent just over three months together during an exceptionally challenging period. He was able to shine a light on my professional life in a unique way which enabled me to capitalise on my strengths and highlight areas for development. Matt's Leadership Pathfinder Model is a fantastic framework for anyone looking to orientate their inner compass and find their true north.

Joshua Bradbury
– Demand Manager, SAP

Matt was/is phenomenal. He is exceptionally easy to talk to and provides exceptional coaching. If my wife noticed a change then you know he's good. Highly recommend to anyone looking to advance their careers.

Luke Galindo
–MD Texas Med Clinic

"Matt, thank you so much for the wonderful coaching over the last few months. With a high degree of empathy, you managed to align my inner compass needle to my true north and gave me the tools and confidence to keep this course. This clarity will undoubtedly help me in all facets of my life from here."

Lars Ohlsen
– Partner Ecosystem Success
– Partner Solution Adoption, SAP

Hmmmm. Not sure a few words will do this man justice. I've worked beside Matt co-facilitating a workshop and he's exceptional. He reads the room and responds. He knows his stuff and how to ply his trade. Flawlessly. Then there's the times that we get to catch up as only a pair of Brits far from home and essentially in the same field can. And I find myself frequently on the other end of the coaching relationship. Matt gets to the heart. And quickly. He has the knack to create the safe space, meets you where you are and moves you forward. Brilliantly. I have no hesitation in recommending Mr. Guiver as executive coach, trainer, facilitator, speaker and writer.

Ron J. West
– Executive coach & creator
of the Chrysalis Program®

Printed in Great Britain
by Amazon

84852858R00099